ALL ABOARD!

The

CANADIAN ROCKIES BY TRAIN

DAVID J. MITCHELL

DOUGLAS & McINTYRE

VANCOUVER / TORONTO

For Madi and Jane

Douglas & McIntyre Ltd.
1615 Venables Street
Vancouver, British Columbia V5L 2H1

Canadian Cataloguing in Publication Data
Mitchell, David J. (David Joseph), 1954-
   All aboard!
   ISBN 1-55054-188-9 pb
   ISBN 1-55054-419-5 cl
1. Railroads—Rocky Mountains (B.C. and Alta.)—History.*
2. Rocky Mountains (B.C. and Alta.)—History.* I. Title
HE2810.C2M57 1995   385'.06'571   C95-910011-3

Editing by Saeko Usukawa
Design by DesignGeist
Cover photograph of "The Rocky Mountaineer"
   crossing the Stoney Creek Bridge by Craig Dollick
Page one photograph of Cathedral Crags in Yoho National Park by Doug Leighton
Printed and bound in Hong Kong by C & C Offset Printing Co. Ltd.

The publisher gratefully acknowledges the assistance of the Canada Council
and the British Columbia Ministry of Tourism, Small Business, and Culture for
its publishing programs.

C O N T E N T S

M A P S

During the course of a busy life, the opportunity to unwind on a truly magnificent train ride is an all-too-rare experience. The chance to think and write about such a journey is a very special joy.

No single volume could possibly tell the complete story of the conception, construction and operation of railways through the Canadian Rockies. My hope is that this book will serve as an accessible and informative introduction to a truly amazing saga. While the emphasis here is given to the first great rail line built by Canadian Pacific, it is my intention to provide a more comprehensive account of the Canadian National story as well as a detailed mile-post route guide in future volumes.

My first thanks must go to Peter Armstrong, the visionary president of the Great Canadian Railtour Company, who encouraged me to take on this project. Peter is a classic entrepreneur who richly deserves the great success that he and "The Rocky Mountaineer" are now enjoying.

A number of employees of the Great Canadian Railtour Company must also be recognized for the courtesies extended to me while researching and writing this volume. The rail car attendants, head office staff and virtually everyone else associated with the train are a credit to a fine young company providing a unique service that, for most of their customers, constitutes the travel experience of a lifetime. I particularly wish to note the kind assistance of Lori Biglow, Dean Wilkins and Tracey Whiting.

A former employee of the company also needs to be acknowledged: Rick Antonson helped lay a firm foundation for "The Rocky Mountaineer," and he also provided a spark of initiative for this book.

In addition, my thanks are also extended to the staff of the various western Canadian archives, museums and libraries who assisted me in my research and helped identify the historic black-and-white photographs which form an important part of the book.

Last, but never least, I offer my heartfelt thanks to Marlene Mitchell, who assisted with the photo research, helped select the stories and anecdotes used from other sources and whose special efforts ensured that the manuscript was completed on time.

A number of copyright holders kindly granted permission to include excerpts from their works in Chapter Four of this book. I hereby gratefully acknowledge them as well:

"The Major's Bath" by Tom Wilson, from *Trail Blazer of the Canadian Rockies* (Calgary: Glenbow-Alberta Institute, 1972). Reprinted by permission of the publisher.

Pierre Berton, *The National Dream: The Great Railway, 1871-1881* and *The Last Spike: The Great Railway, 1881-1885* (Toronto: McClelland & Stewart, 1970 and 1971). Reprinted by permission of the author.

"Memories of Dr. Hector and the Kicking Horse" by Peter Erasmus from *Buffalo Days and Nights* (Calgary: Glenbow-Alberta Institute, 1976). Reprinted by permission of the publisher.

"The Glacier Slide: Bill LaChance" from Robert D. Turner, ed., *Railroaders: Recollections from the Steam Era in British Columbia* (Sound Heritage No. 31, 1981, Provincial Archives of British Columbia). Permission granted by the B.C. Archives and Records Service.

"A Tale of Three Bears" from J. F. Garden, *Nicholas Morant's Canadian Pacific* (Revelstoke: Footprint Publishing, 1991). Reprinted by permission of the publisher.

"High Wire Artists" from Ken Liddell, *I'll Take the Train* (Saskatoon: Western Producer Prairie Books, 1977). Reprinted by permission of the author's estate.

"By Car and Cowcatcher" by Agnes Macdonald from *Murray's Magazine*, Volume 1, January-June 1887, London, England.

David J. Mitchell
Vancouver

The Promise of Railroads

"I travel not to go anywhere, but to go.
I travel for travel's sake. The great affair is to move."

—Robert Louis Stevenson

Throughout history, people have always harboured the desire to visit distant regions or foreign lands. From ancient times through to the Middle Ages, travel by foot and by beast of burden were the predominant modes of transport, although harnessing the power of the wind allowed sailing craft to explore the seas and oceans within a limited range. The invention of the compass freed mariners to open up navigation routes, leading to astonishing voyages of discovery. Commerce and empire were the primary forces propelling small sailing vessels over the horizon and into the unknown. "Here be dragons," noted early cartographers in the margins of their crude maps of vast seas and mysterious faraway lands.

It is important to remember that the word "travel" comes from the French word travail, "work." Only in the last century or so have people travelled for pleasure. Prior to that, travel was hard and dangerous work, and very few contemplated setting out on a real journey. Such adventures were reserved for those hearty or driven souls intent on pursuing trade, pilgrimages or war.

Land travel was particularly arduous. In medieval times, for example, it could take up to four months to complete the journey from London to Rome. The gruelling trip followed rough routes marked by cart tracks. In strange and often hostile environments, travellers were subject to unscrupulous innkeepers and marauding bandits. Later, in the seventeenth and eighteenth centuries, it was both unconventional and courageous to go on an extended journey by foot or by horseback around even one's own country. It is difficult to imagine anyone in those days travelling "for travel's sake" as Robert Louis Stevenson later advised.

However, in the nineteenth century, the Industrial Revolution transformed both attitudes and abilities to travel. And the single most important development was the invention and application of the steam engine. Steam locomotives for the purpose of transport appeared in Britain early in the nineteenth century, and the first railway, between Stockton and Darlington, marked a turning point in the history of travel. The first passengers on that line may not have fully realized the import of their adventure on September 27, 1825, but the scene was described by an onlooker who noted that most "did not the night before sleep a wink…The happy faces of many, the vacant stare of astonishment of others, and the alarm depicted on the countenance of some, gave variety to the picture."

When the Duke of Wellington learned of the reality of the steam locomotive, he said: "I see no reason to suppose that these machines will ever force themselves into general use." Of course, the grand old duke—who illustrated the reactionary response of many people to this new form of travel—was wrong. Just a couple of decades later, a network of railways covered Europe. This was the heroic age of European railway building and represented a revolution in land travel that soon spread around the world.

At first, railways were stubbornly resisted, especially by those who had existing interests in roads and canals: coachmakers, harnessmakers, horse dealers and innkeepers feared they would be put out of business. The aristocracy had other concerns: the first attempt to get a bill through Parliament permitting the construction of a railroad between Liverpool and Manchester failed because one duke protested that it would spoil his fox covers.

Nevertheless, Britain led the way in rail transport. By 1838 there were 500 miles of railroad in England and Wales, and in 1850 there were 6,621 miles in operation. This burgeoning new enterprise stimulated a corresponding revolution in heavy industries, especially in mining and metallurgy, since railroads created huge new demands for coal and iron.

Railways quickly emerged as big businesses, encouraging the rise of big contractors. In a single generation, this great new industry offered employment to thousands, ranging from the gangs of navvies who laid the tracks to the drivers, firemen and other staff who ran the lines. Moreover, the fears of large-scale unemployment among those who worked on roads and canals proved unfounded.

Among the new businesses resulting from the development of railways were passenger excursions, like those organized in the 1840s by Thomas Cook in England. Nothing quite like this had ever happened before. Round-trip fare for the first such excursion in 1841, covering what was regarded as the enormous distance of 11 miles there and back, was a shilling—half price for children. The well-organized event, which attracted 570 paying passengers to Leicester station, was so unusual that "people crowded the streets, filled the windows, covered the housetops, and cheered us all along the line, with the heartiest welcome," wrote Cook afterwards.

Thomas Cook and others wanted to make rail travel available to people of all classes—not only the elite of society. Besides, it was also good business. Rail travel was not, however, without risks and dangers, especially in the early years. Rail passengers travelling in open cars found themselves showered with burning embers from the tall funnels of the coal-burning locomotives. At the next stop they would leap down and rush to any available source of water to douse their burning clothes.

The trials, tribulations and accomplishments of British railway pioneers helped the transportation revolution to spread far afield. Initially, the Belgians set the pace on the Continent, with a rail line from Brussels to Malines carrying more than half a million passengers in 1835, its first year of operation. The French were slower to embrace the new technology and by mid-century had only some 2,000 miles of rail, a third as much as Britain, which was half the size of France. Perhaps the greatest impact of railroads in Europe was felt in Germany, a poor, backward country that was abruptly shaken out of its traditional outlooks and habits. The first German railway opened in 1835 in Bavaria. When a line was completed from Leipzig to Dresden in 1839, it carried 412,000 people in its initial year. Some female passengers held needles in their mouths to prevent unwanted familiarity in the darkness of the line's single tunnel. The iron tracks opened up rural areas of Germany and led the way to an industrial expansion that enabled it to become the centre of a continental system of transport and distribution.

Nineteenth-century Europe was transformed by the railway, which reduced the travel time between destinations by more than ten times that of the horse-and-buggy era. Europe was divided into small countries whose boundaries had been drawn in the age of horses and roads. Railways, therefore, increased the congestion within an already crowded continent that was now effectively reduced in size by the revolution wrought by the steam engine.

This was not be the case elsewhere. The promise of railways in other parts of the world, especially on continents not yet industrialized nor densely populated and where political boundaries were not yet tightly drawn, was almost limitless. Likewise, the prospect of laying tracks over vast new distances was enough to inspire dreams of riches, dreams of empire and dreams of nationhood.

Soon the romance of rail travel encircled the globe. The haunting sound of an engine's whistle echoing through the mountains at night, the thundering drive across the plains, the amazing restraint of the powerful locomotives as they edged their way in and out of great cathedral-like stations and lonely frontier outposts made them the inspiration of poets, composers and filmmakers.

Once on board a train and moving down the track, the excitement and anticipation of the platform left behind, you are captivated by the world rolling by. You can see so much more from a train than other forms of travel, and nothing else gives you a sense of covering distance, of miles passing beneath the wheels. And, as the great twentieth-century rail traveller Paul Theroux wrote: "Almost anything is possible in a train."

Ultimately, that is the promise of railroads.

Dream of a Nation

Today, on the verge of the twenty-first century, it is difficult to fully appreciate just how revolutionary it once was to lay steel rails on the ground for long distances and over them run heavy steam engines that pulled cars filled with passengers and freight. As basic, even primitive, as this may now seem, in the nineteenth century railways represented a massive shift in how people viewed travel, distances and the possibilities for growth, development and expansion.

The initial British railway mania spread not only to Europe but throughout the world, finding its fullest expression and realizing its greatest potential in North America. Even though Europeans led in the settlement of this "New World," railroads helped ensure that North America would never become another Europe. The small nations that divided Western Europe had been carved out as political

Opposite page:
**VANCOUVER TO KAMLOOPS
The lower Fraser Canyon
with an exceptionally big
ponderosa pine at right.**
Ed Gifford

Canada's First Railroad

The first railroad in what is now Canada opened for business near Montréal in the summer of 1836. The Champlain and St. Lawrence, as it was called, employed a small imported English locomotive known affectionately as "Kitten," a toy when compared with the hulking, powerful engines that would later haul passengers and freight across the northern portion of the continent. The Champlain and St. Lawrence carried its cargo about 12 miles to St. Jean-sur-Richelieu. From there, passengers and commodities were floated down Lake Champlain by steamer to connect with American railroads. Up to that time, Canadians had been content to ship people and produce by water or overland on horse-drawn wagons, until winter came, paralysing all traffic and trade.

and administrative units in the days when foot and horse were the only methods of transportation and communication. In North America, however, the dream of transcontinental nations, stretching from the Atlantic through a sprawling western frontier to the Pacific, was made possible largely because of the advent of railroads. Indeed, had North American settlement spread westward across the continent by means of only horse power and wagon roads, such dreams could never have been realized. Railways, however, played the role of a great unifier, allowing for a new kind of nation, sustained on a grander scale than would otherwise have been possible or imaginable.

The young, aggressive nation of the United States was quick to take up the new technology of railway transportation. By the middle of the nineteenth century, Americans could already boast of 2,000 miles of track. Unfortunately, railways did not come soon enough to help avert the deepening conflict of interests and ideas that led to the outbreak of the American Civil War. However, when that great conflagration was over, the United States eagerly turned its attention to westward expansion—and railways became the biggest business in the country. By 1865 there were 35,000 miles of steam railroads in operation and transcontinental railways became the most spectacular achievement of the postwar era.

When the Central Pacific and the Union Pacific joined rails with a golden spike near Great Salt Lake on May 10, 1869, the first transcontinental rail link was complete. The boldness of that accomplishment was reflected in the optimism of an expanding American empire. Anticipating the completion of that first great iron band across the continent, a San Francisco newspaper, the *Daily Alta California*, declared: "That the U.S. are bound finally to absorb all the world and the rest of mankind, every well-regulated American mind is prepared to admit. When the fever is on our people do not seem to know when and where to stop, but keep on swallowing, so long as there is anything in reach."

Several other American railways were also reaching their respective ways across the land, eventually to embrace the Pacific coast as well. Not only did these transcontinental lines ensure that the United States would settle and develop all of its territories from coast to coast but their amazing success suggested that the Americans might be actively reaching for their self-proclaimed "Manifest Destiny" of incorporating all of North America within their boundaries.

A steam engine pulls a train through a snowy mountain landscape.
Whyte Museum of the
Canadian Rockies V227 2865

To the north, however, a number of small British colonies were conspiring to prevent the fulfilment of such a destiny—and, ironically, railroads played a decisive role. Initially, however, British North Americans were comparatively slow to seize upon the promise of railways.

By the end of the 1840s the Americans had built more than 8,000 miles of railroads, whereas the northern colonies could count just 66 miles of track. This frustrated those British colonists who expounded the virtues of railways, believing them to be the only method to liberate them from their frozen winters of inactivity. T. C. Keefer, a Montréal engineer, delivered a lecture in 1849—"The Philosophy of Railroads"—that effectively summarized this strong sense of frustration:

VANCOUVER TO KAMLOOPS
Cisco Crossings (Mile 101)
over the Fraser River near
Lytton, B.C.
Hugh Martell

Opposite page:
VANCOUVER TO KAMLOOPS
A few miles east of Lytton,
a train has emerged from
a tunnel and passed
through three rock sheds
at Avalanche Alley (also
called White Canyon),
on the Thompson River.
Hugh Martell

The Search for the Northwest Passage

Ever since Marco Polo's successful land expedition to the Far East in the thirteenth century, Europeans had been seeking an elusive ocean route to the Orient. In fact, the discovery of the Americas was the direct consequence of early efforts to reach Asia by sea. While successful seafaring voyages to China via the Cape of Good Hope and Cape Horn were eventually made, the long and treacherous nature of such journeys forced a number of navigators to search for a more direct route, a passage through North America. In the late eighteenth century, the north Pacific coast of North America was explored by Captain James Cook, Britain's master navigator,

Old winter is once more upon us, and our inland seas are "dreary and inhospitable wastes" to the merchant and the traveller;—our rivers are sealed fountains—and an embargo which no human power can remove is laid on all our ports. Around our deserted wharves and warehouses are huddled the naked spars—the blasted forests of trade—from which the sails have fallen like the leaves of autumn. The splashing wheels are silenced—the roar of the steam is hushed—the gay saloon, so lately thronged with busy life, is now but an abandoned hall—and the cold snow revels in solitary possession of the untrodden deck. The animation of business is suspended, the life blood of commerce is curdled and stagnant in the St. Lawrence—the great aorta of the North. On land, the heavy stage labours through mingled frost and mud in the West—or struggles through drifted snow, and slides with uncertain track over the icy hills of Eastern Canada. Far away to the South is heard the daily scream of the steam whistle—but from Canada there is no escape: blockaded and imprisoned by Ice and Apathy, we have at least ample time for reflection—and if there be comfort in Philosophy may we not profitably consider the PHILOSOPHY OF RAILROADS.

Keefer's clarion call for British North Americans to embrace rail travel was timely and well heeded. The eastern colonies of Nova Scotia, New Brunswick and Canada soon became infected with the new "philosophy." Joseph Howe, a prominent Nova Scotian and later a Father of Canadian Confederation, boldly predicted to a Halifax audience: "I am neither a prophet nor the son of a prophet, but I believe that many in this room will live to hear the whistle of the steam engine in the passes of the Rocky Mountains and make the journey from Halifax to the Pacific in five or six days."

Of course, the problems faced by the British North American colonists included more than icy northern winters. The colonies were sparsely populated and relatively isolated when compared with their expansion-minded American neighbours. Moreover, the eastern colonies were separated from the small Pacific coast settlement on Vancouver Island by a vast continent with a few settlers and native peoples spread out over the rugged Precambrian Shield, the immense prairies and beyond the intimidating obstacle of the Rockies. In addition, the large amount of capital required to finance railway construction was in short supply. This changed in 1849 with the passage of the Railway Guarantee Act, which encouraged any railroad more than 75 miles in length to borrow money for financing—with the interest on the loan guaranteed by the government. Soon there was a deluge of applications for railway charters and the 1850s saw the colonies finally seized in the grip of a strong case of railway fever.

Although the initial burst of railway construction was concentrated in the eastern colonies, the dream of a transcontinental railroad linking all of British North America lived on. However, it is important to understand where this dream originated. The inspiration for it did not come from a desire to open up the west or to settle the interior of the continent or to bond with fellow British colonists in Victoria. Rather, it was the lure of the Orient. The age-old European goal of discovering a passage through North America for trade access to the riches of Asia was finding new expression in the proposals for a rail connection across Britain's North American possessions. By the mid-nineteenth century, when the British had annexed Hong Kong and developed it as a major entrepôt, a land route across North America seemed a logical alternative to the fading dream of a northwest sea passage to Asia.

Of course, native peoples had inhabited what is now western Canada for thousands of years prior to the arrival of Europeans. A great diversity of aboriginal groups lived on both sides of the towering mountain ranges separating the west coast from the interior plains. But was there a land route through that mountain barrier?

Explorers by land did indeed have more success crossing the continent. In fact, the story of transportation to the west coast begins with the journeys of the great fur trader and explorer Alexander Mackenzie. In 1789, searching for a land route to the Pacific, he explored what he called the "River of Disappointment"—later named the Mackenzie River in his honour—which flows north into the Bering Sea. Travelling overland, Mackenzie finally reached the Pacific coast on July 22, 1793—missing Captain George Vancouver at Bella Coola Inlet by only a few days. Other prominent explorers of the fur trade era, such as Simon Fraser and David Thompson, followed Mackenzie's lead. As a result, by the early years of the nineteenth century, it had been clearly established that it was possible—albeit extremely challenging—to forge a transportation route between the established colonies in the east and the few early settlers on the British Pacific coast.

A number of dreamers convinced themselves—and sought to con-

who concluded that there was no Northwest Passage by sea from the Pacific to the Atlantic. Accompanying Cook on that historic voyage was George Vancouver, who a decade and a half later was commissioned by the British government to return to the west coast of North America to determine yet again if there was a possible passage. Vancouver carefully charted the coastline, but his survey concluded in 1794 with a report that there was no obvious sea passage inland to the interior of the continent. The long-sought sea route was finally abandoned after Sir John Franklin's expedition via the Arctic in two specially outfitted ships met with disaster in 1847. Recent examinations of the remains of crew members have revealed the grisly truth that they resorted to cannibalism while waiting in vain for rescue.

VANCOUVER TO KAMLOOPS
West of Kamloops, a Canadian
National freight train runs along
the dramatic weathered sand-
stone slopes of Kamloops Lake.
Photo CN

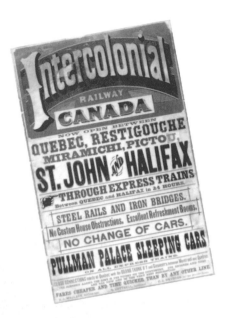

vince others—of the feasibility of a railroad across British North America to link Britain with its colonies in Asia via a new, shorter and more efficient transportation route. Perhaps it was the optimism of the Victorian age, or simply irrepressible confidence in the new railway technology, that spurred these dreamers on—for none of them had ever actually traversed the forbidding expanse of the northern continent.

As early as 1829, before any railways were in operation in the New World, Sir Richard Bonnycastle, an officer of the Royal Engineers, suggested the idea of a railway connection from coast to coast. Bonnycastle, who later published a book called *Canada and the Canadians*, wrote: "We shall yet place an iron belt from the Atlantic to the Pacific, a railroad from Halifax to Nootka Sound, and thus reach China in a pleasure voyage."

Another hard-headed British army engineer, Robert Carmichael-Smyth, writing in the late 1840s, envisaged a "Grand National Railway" which would be "the means of enabling vessels steaming from our magnificent colonies . . . all carrying the rich products of the East to land them at the commencement of the West—to be forwarded and distributed throughout our North American provinces and delivered within thirty days to the ports of Great Britain."

Bonnycastle, Carmichael-Smyth and a host of other visionaries, poets and pamphleteers from this era, attracted by the mighty lure of the Orient, saw an opportunity for Britain's imperial and commercial interests to unite the northern portion of North America with a single, bold rail line.

As the railway boom of the 1850s reached the eastern British colonies, a Toronto mining promoter and lawyer, Allan Macdonell, argued that if the Egyptians could build pyramids, then colonists could build a railway across 3,000 miles of largely unexplored territory. He applied for a charter to undertake a transcontinental rail line, which he described as: "The shortest, cheapest and safest communication for Europe and all Asia." Macdonell was turned down, his proposal being both premature and too grandiose to seriously consider at that time. Reaction from the United States, however, showed that he was on the right track. On March 27, 1851, the *New York Tribune* reported:

> A route through British North America is in some respects even preferable to that through our own territory. Having its Atlantic seaport at Halifax and its Pacific depot near Vancouver's Island, it would inevitably

draw to it the commerce of Europe, Asia and the United States, so thus, British America, from a mere colonial dependency, would assume a controlling rank in the world. To her, other nations would be tributary, and in vain would the United States attempt to be her rival; for we could never dispute with her the possession of the Asiatic commerce, or the power which that commerce confers.

In truth, the Americans need not have been overly concerned. Even with encouragement from their Mother Country, the British colonies were in no position to quickly capitalize on the opportunity correctly foreseen. In fact, when it came to railway building or economic development, it was difficult for British North Americans to compete with their much larger, energetic neighbour to the south. That fact, however, and the fear which accompanied it, would have significant repercussions for the national dream that was now stirring.

The idea of the small British colonies uniting to form a new, independent country was made feasible by the growing networks of railways that promised to bind them together physically in a way that only a few had dreamed possible. By 1860, the Grand Trunk, the colonies' foremost railway, had about 1,000 miles of track laid along the St. Lawrence River and the shores of the Great Lakes. Numerous other rail lines were also winding their way through this region; few of them were profitable and almost all of them had strong connections to prominent politicians of the day.

Close ties between railways and politics

A steam locomotive emerging from a tunnel.
Whyte Museum of the
Canadian Rockies
V263 NA71-1581

The Adams River Sockeye Salmon Run

One of nature's most fascinating mysteries takes place along the banks of the Adams River in the heart of British Columbia's Shuswap Lake region. Every four years, around September, over a million salmon—one of the the world's largest salmon runs—journey 305 miles up the Fraser River to its tributary, the Adams River.

During their journey home, the silvery salmon change colour to a deep red. Once they spawn, the fish die.

In March, the eggs hatch into tiny alevins and grow into fry. Of the 800 million fry that leave the Adams River, only 200 million will survive to travel down the Fraser to the Pacific Ocean. For the next two and a half years, the salmon travel through the North Pacific, then return home to the Adams River to begin the cycle all over again.

Opposite page:
KAMLOOPS TO BANFF
Sockeye salmon spawning on the Adams River near Squilax, B.C., in the early autumn.
Doug Leighton

had already become a Canadian tradition. As early as the 1850s, it was charged that the Grand Trunk Railway, not the government, really ran the colonies. The Toronto *Globe* editorialized on April 22, 1857: "The Grand Trunk governs Canada at the present moment. Its power is paramount. The Ministry are mere puppets in its hands and dance whatever tune the Company pipes."

In spite of such controversy, the railway boom continued almost unabated. The concept of an intercolonial railroad linking the eastern colonies became the focus of much heated debate in the 1860s. Indeed, the intercolonial line played a large part in the discussions leading up to the union of the eastern colonies in a new Canadian Confederation. Some critics even suggested that confederation was actually a political manoeuvre to save the intercolonial railway!

The British North America Act, which formed the basis for Canada's constitution, was proclaimed in the country's new capital, Ottawa, on July 1, 1867. Section 145 of the act states that "the construction of the Intercolonial Railway is essential to the Consolidation of the Union of British North America." This may well be the only written national constitution that specifically mandates the construction of a major rail line as a precondition to the birth of a new nation. However, it accurately foretold the crucial role that railways would play in the first decades of the new country's history.

Canadian Confederation coincided with and helped precipitate a series of events and bold strokes that, surprisingly, within a few years led to a complete consolidation of national boundaries in North America. One of the dominant themes of this era, and a great motivating force, was a fear of American expansion into the northwest portion of the continent. For the fledgling Canadians, this fear seemed well justified. On the very day that Queen Victoria signed the British North America Act, the Americans were placing the finishing touches on the Alaska Purchase Treaty. This remarkable concurrence was seen by many Canadians as more than mere coincidence. In fact, the purchase of Alaska from Russia by the United States was considered to be a flanking movement to confederation as well as a threat to Canadian expansion westward to the Pacific. As such, the acquisition appeared to hang a cloud over Canada's future.

British and Canadian statesmen of this period believed that if Canada was to survive on a continent dominated by the Americans, it too would

The Hudson's Bay Company

In the seventeenth century, the New World (America) was a land rich in wildlife with vast forests and pristine waters that were a natural habitat for many fur-bearing animals. The most sought-after of these was the beaver, to fill the steady demand in Europe for luxury hats made of beaver fur.

In 1667, Prince Rupert, a cousin of King Charles II of England, formed a group of investors to enter into the fur trade. The group came to be known as the Hudson's Bay Company and was granted a royal charter that gave it control of a vast area (now part of Canada) of 1,486,000 square miles. The territory the company controlled came to be called Rupert's Land.

need to become a transcontinental nation. Canada would have to expand westward, consolidating the Pacific coast and the colony of British Columbia as well as the vast area in between, Rupert's Land, which was still controlled by the Hudson's Bay Company. Canadian apprehension over the U.S. purchase of Alaska was only compounded when the Americans completed their first transcontinental rail line within two years of the Alaska acquisition.

Rather than hastening the Manifest Destiny of the United States, these acts of expansion actually gave impetus and focus to a Canadian destiny—even though it was not quite manifest at the time. Indeed, it must have seemed ambitious in the extreme. The United States had a rapidly growing population of 40 million, with almost a million American citizens living on the Pacific coast. By contrast, Canada was a small country of about three-and-a-half million souls, with only a few thousand non-native settlers in the west and British Columbia. Immediate consolidation of half a continent seemed highly improbable.

One Father of Confederation said that it was a "burlesque" to speak of a Canada stretching across the west to the Pacific Ocean, when the thousands of miles separating British Columbia from the eastern centres of population were almost empty and without communication except through the United States or around Cape Horn. For Canada's first prime minister, John A. Macdonald, the aggressiveness of American expansionism only emphasized what a huge and unmanageable inconvenience the British northwest represented: "I would be quite willing personally to leave the whole country a wilderness for the next half-century, but I fear if Englishmen do not go there, Yankees will."

At the time of Canadian Confederation and the American purchase of Alaska, British Columbia was not much more than a bunch of lonely frontier outposts with a non-native population of less than ten thousand. But the greatest problem facing British Columbia was isolation. Great Britain was virtually at the other end of the earth. Canada was more than 3,000 miles away and separated from the colony by an intimidating geography. To the west, the nearest British colony was across the Pacific in Hong Kong. And the only foreign intercourse easily available to British Columbia was with American settlers in Washington, Oregon and California. San Francisco was the colony's closest link with the outside world and, to a large degree, U.S. steamship lines were dominating commercial trade on the west coast of the continent. British Columbia's future seemed increasingly to be with the United States. Certainly, north-south connections along the Pacific coast appeared stronger and much more natural than any far-fetched east-west axis.

In the United States, much of the reaction to the purchase of Alaska was focussed specifically on the isolated British colony, and the American press cast eager glances in the colony's direction. The *St. Paul Daily Press* declared that British Columbia was wedded to the United States by "geographical affinities which no human power can put asunder as He has divided it from Canada by physical barriers which no human power can overcome." The *New York Herald* suggested that "the people of this country will certainly find it inconvenient to have different portions of our republican empire separated by foreign territory." And another New York newspaper, the *World,* argued on almost completely aesthetic grounds: "A gap in our possessions on the Pacific Coast will always be an eyesore to the nation, whose sense of symmetry will be offended by the ragged coastline."

British Columbians were gripped by confusion. On one hand, Victoria's *British Colonist* newspaper bemoaned the fact that the purchase of Alaska by the United States "places the whole of Her Majesty's possessions on the Pacific in the position of a piece of meat between two slices of bread, where they can be devoured in a single bite." On the other hand, Americans residing in the colony rejoiced by hanging U.S. flags out their windows in triumph. Great Britain, however, had no intention of ceding any portion of her empire to the United States and made a concerted effort to encourage the union of all her North American territories with Canada. Speedily, almost hastily, the gears were set in motion for the creation of a second transcontinental North American nation.

In 1868 the British Parliament passed an act allowing for the liquidation of the rights of the Hudson's Bay Company and the transfer of Rupert's Land to Canada. However, one of the greatest legal transfers of territory and sovereignty in history was conducted like a mere real estate transaction. In its hurry to gain control of the huge area, the Canadian government failed to acknowledge the existence of its inhabitants—native people and white settlers—who were not even officially notified of the land transfer. In 1869 the Canadian-appointed governor was met by armed resistance at Red River, led by the Metis (French and British half-breeds), guided by the exceptional abilities of Louis Riel. The government of

Following pages:
**KAMLOOPS TO BANFF
A creek running through cedar and hemlock rainforest in the interior of British Columbia.**
Scott Rowed

Canada was fearful that the United States would take advantage of this acutely embarrassing incident and, as a result, quickly resolved the Red River Rebellion by negotiating on the terms and conditions of the Metis and other settlers. In 1870 Rupert's Land was officially taken over by Canada and, in satisfying the demands of the Red River settlers, the Canadian government created a new province: Manitoba.

The way was now clear for union with British Columbia. In 1869 a new governor for the colony was appointed, Anthony Musgrave, with explicit instructions to pave the way for British Columbia's entry into confederation. There was no overwhelming public sentiment for such a move within the colony. After all, Canada was on the other side of the continent and, furthermore, a petition had been circulating throughout British Columbia calling for annexation to the United States. Nevertheless, Governor Musgrave did his duty.

In March 1870 the colony agreed upon terms of union with Canada. The delegation that was appointed to meet with Canadian negotiators travelled to far-off Ottawa via steamship to San Francisco and then by American railways, which enabled them to arrive at their destination in a few days rather than the month-long journey it would have been.

Once in Ottawa, the British Columbians discovered that Canada was so anxious to include their colony within its boundaries that it was prepared to go beyond the terms requested by the colonists. The British Columbians had hoped for a promise of a wagon road to be built from Canada across the prairies, through the mountains and eventually to the Pacific coast. George Etienne Cartier, Prime Minister John A. Macdonald's French-Canadian lieutenant, pulled the small delegation aside and advised them to request a railway; he was sure they would receive such a commitment. It was the first of many, many instances when British Columbians would be shown how to extract promises from the federal government by craftier Québec politicians.

Upon their return home, the British Columbia delegation was greeted enthusiastically. Not only had they agreed upon the terms of union with Canada but they had obtained a firm promise of a transcontinental railway connecting them to the Atlantic Ocean. The terms of the agreement read as follows:

The Government of the Dominion undertake to secure the commencement simultaneously, within two years of the date of union, of the construction of a railway from the Pacific towards the Rocky Mountains and from such point as may be selected east of the Rocky Mountains towards the Pacific, to connect the seaboard of British Columbia with the railway system of Canada; and further to secure the completion of such railway within ten years from the date of union.

The agreement was ratified by the colony in January of 1871, and later that year British Columbia became the sixth province in confederation. Canada had at last become a transcontinental nation. However, it was a tenuous union that defied both geography and economics.

Only a railway, it seemed, could truly fulfil the promise of a new nation, but no one knew exactly what route such a rail line would follow or, indeed, if its construction over the immense western terrain was even feasible. In Ottawa, opponents of the government, with logic in their favour, declared the promise of a railway to British Columbia to be "a preposterous proposition" and an act of "insane recklessness." But Prime Minister John A. Macdonald and his colleagues had emotion on their side. They believed that Canada could not grow into a nation, in the truest sense of the word, without being bound together by the magical tie of a railroad. It was that bold dream of nationhood that would give birth to a Canadian railway through the Rocky Mountains.

Towards the Last Spike

Visitors to western Canada are usually eager to see the Rocky Mountains. To travellers who approach them from the east, the Rockies are unmistakable. After vast expanses of rolling plains come the foothills, which suddenly give way to the towering, snow-capped peaks of legend and lore. However, the approach from the west— while no less dramatic—requires some orientation. Visitors to Vancouver, for instance, often mistake the Coast Mountains for the Rockies. In fact, it is necessary to journey inland through several other mountain ranges—including the Monashees, Selkirks and Pur- cells—before travellers can behold the majesty of the Canadian Rockies. All of these ranges run on a north-south axis, with the Rockies roughly forming the southern boundary between British Columbia and Alberta.

Opposite page:
KAMLOOPS TO BANFF East of Revelstoke, on the Illecillewaet River. The Sir Donald Range is in the background, with Mount Sir Donald itself on the right.
Doug Leighton

The Rocky Mountains were moulded over a span of time that defies human comprehension. Their story is not one of thundering volcanoes and burning lava flows but, rather, a tale of ancient oceans, slow movements of the earth's crust and the inexorable grinding of massive glaciers. Geologists estimate that the oldest rock in the Canadian Rockies was formed over 600 million years ago, and fossils indicate that this mountainous region once constituted an ocean shoreline. Starting around 200 million years ago, most of what is now western Canada was pushed up above the surface of the ocean by powerful geological forces that created the mountain ranges. A comparatively recent event of the last two million years was the sculpting of the Rockies by enormous glaciers, which advanced and retreated during four major ice ages. These giant glaciers—some of which measured 2400 metres (8,000 feet) in thickness—significantly shaped the faces and peaks of the mountain ranges we know today.

Native peoples were the first humans to see the Rocky Mountains. Archaeological evidence suggests that they hunted, travelled and lived on

The steep walls of the infamous Hell's Gate Canyon on the Fraser River, 23 miles above Yale, B.C., c. 1867. Racks of drying salmon can be seen along the canyon's side.
B.C. Archives and Records Service 10230 A3874

both sides of the Canadian Rockies at least 11,000 years ago. While native groups on the Pacific coast were relatively settled, those in the interior mountain regions were frequently on the move, in search of better hunting and living conditions. Some, like the Kootenays of southeastern B.C., were related to natives of the plains, on the other side of the Rockies. Historical estimates of the native population vary, but there is no doubt that the First Nations of western Canada were made up of a number of different groups and cultures. In British Columbia, the native population outnumbered white settlers until the eve of the twentieth century.

The first recorded instance of a white person sighting the Rockies was in 1754, when fur trader Anthony Henday glimpsed what he called "The Shining Mountains" from near present-day Red Deer, Alberta. Over time, the fur traders established a few arduous routes through the Rockies. In the early years of the nineteenth century, following in the footsteps of Alexander Mackenzie, Simon Fraser, another great explorer of the fur-trade era, commanded a historic expedition across the Rockies to the Pacific. He established trading posts which became the first permanent white settlements west of the Rocky Mountains. While searching for a navigable waterway to the Pacific, Simon Fraser encountered the confluence of the "muddy waters" and the "clear waters" known today as the Fraser and Thompson Rivers. His expedition by canoe and by land followed the often-treacherous route of the Fraser Canyon. After viewing the section of the canyon later called "Hell's Gate," Simon Fraser noted in his diary: "I have been for a long period among the Rocky Mountains, but I have never seen anything like this country. It is so wild that I cannot find words to describe our situation at times. We had to pass where no human being should venture."

Fraser believed he was following the Columbia River, but when he eventually arrived at its mouth on the Pacific, he realized he had actually been travelling down a great unknown river, too dangerous to be of much use to the fur trade. His contemporary, explorer and geographer David Thompson, named the river after Fraser, who had already named the river of "clear waters" after Thompson. These mutual admirers and adventurous surveyors not only did much for the fur trade but also helped achieve an understanding of the difficult terrain on both sides of the Rocky Mountains. David Thompson, who has been described as "the greatest geographer of all time," explored and mapped the southern portions of the

Hell's Gate

Hell's Gate is the narrowest part of the Fraser River. Over 200 million gallons of water pound and surge through the gorge every minute, creating rapids that flow at a speed of up to 25 miles per hour.

Historically, the Fraser River was home to huge salmon runs, with as many as 5 million fish swimming up the river to their spawning grounds. In 1914, however, railroad construction blasting and subsequent slides at Hell's Gate blocked most of the river channel and prevented huge numbers of salmon from going upstream.

After 30 years of research, a series of concrete fishways was completed in 1945 to enable spawning salmon to journey upstream. The Fraser River system has now regained its position as the premier salmon river in Canada.

KAMLOOPS TO BANFF
**The famous Rogers Pass
through the Selkirk
Mountains. Trains used
to run through here
before the Connaught
and Macdonald Tunnels
were built.**
Tourism B.C.

Opposite page:
KAMLOOPS TO BANFF
**Snow blowing off the
peak of majestic Mount
Sir Donald.**
Doug Leighton

A portrait of Sandford Fleming, the man in charge of surveying the route for the Canadian Pacific Railway transcontinental line through thousands of miles of wilderness, 1880.
National Archives of Canada PA26664

One of the camels imported during the gold rush era to work on the construction of the Cariboo Road into the interior of British Columbia, c. 1880.
B.C. Archives and Records Service 759 A 347

Canadian Rockies and, with his Metis wife and children, navigated a number of rivers, including the Columbia.

The journeys of these early explorers, charting routes through almost impassable mountains, under extreme weather conditions and amidst often-hostile native Indians, added to the sparse knowledge of the Rockies but did not make travel through them much more accessible.

It was not only the fur trade that inspired penetration of the mountains. In the late 1850s the discovery of gold in British Columbia brought over 30,000 fortune-seekers from around the world in one of the great pioneering gold rushes. Most of that ambitious stream of humanity arrived at the Pacific coast by voyaging over the ocean, then making the difficult overland trek into the interior and the Cariboo goldfields. Crude wagon roads were built from the coast up the Fraser Canyon. And among the beasts of burden used to haul goods and gold were camels, imported into the frontier—an experiment doomed to failure, for their soft hooves could not adapt to the rough, mountainous terrain.

So powerful was the lure of gold that even some people from the eastern colonies were encouraged to attempt the daunting journey across the continent and through the Rockies. One of the great adventures in nineteenth-century travel was thus prompted when a number of groups set out from Ontario and Québec via Red River in search of riches. They became known as the Overlanders, and consisted of about 200 men, one pregnant woman and three small children.

They travelled west in Red River carts, covering the first 1,000 miles or so to Fort Edmonton fairly quickly, averaging two and a half miles an hour. However, much of the remainder of the route was treacherous, without so much as a trail to follow. As they ventured through the Yellowhead Pass and started the dangerous journey south, many of the Overlanders gave up or fell by the wayside. They abandoned their bulky carts, using their horses and oxen as pack animals. Native people would have attacked and slaughtered the determined group, except for the presence of Catherine Schubert and her children. Following the perilous route of the fur traders, the Overlanders were forced to raft down whitewater rivers, losing many of their pack animals and growing ever smaller as a group. In October 1862 an exhausted party of about twenty arrived at Fort Kamloops, where Mrs. Schubert gave birth to the first white child born in the interior of British Columbia. Now, every summer, a raft race is held on the Thompson River from Clearwater to Kamloops, commemorating the bravery of the Overlanders.

The hazardous nature of these pioneering expeditions through the Rockies, remarkable as they were, served only to emphasize the impracticality of east-west travel across the northern portion of the continent. However, the dramatic interplay between people and the mountains during the surveying and construction of the promised Canadian railway brought the Rockies to the attention of the world. When the railway was promised in 1871 as part of the bargain for British Columbia's entry into Canadian Confederation, many doubted that construction would ever actually be completed. Yet, in spite of delays, which were the cause of great anxiety and consternation in British Columbia, by 1885 the transcontinental railroad would become a reality, transforming the mountainous wilds of western Canada from *terra incognita* into a world-famous travel destination.

The first task of the Government of Canada was to undertake a reconnaissance of the route to be followed by the new western railway. The decision was made to place this onerous assignment in the capable hands of Sandford Fleming, one of the most farsighted and talented Canadians of his century. At the time, Fleming was serving as engineer-in-chief for the Intercolonial Railway, linking central Canada with the eastern maritime provinces. But the dictum "If you want a job done, give it to a busy person" seems to have been created with Sandford Fleming in mind. Not only

The Growth of Kamloops

The first inhabitants of the Kamloops area were the Shuswap, a group that is part of the Salish Indian nation. The name Kamloops comes from the Shuswap word kah-moloops, meaning "meeting of the waters," in reference to the fact it is located at the junction of the North and South Thompson River.

In 1811, Americans from the Pacific Fur Company arrived and set up a trading post, followed by their Canadian rivals, the North West Company.

By the 1850s, the gold rush had begun, and miners from all over the world began to flock to the area, hoping to make their fortune.

By 1886, with the completion of the CPR, Kamloops grew quickly and became even more important as a rail centre when the Canadian Northern was built in 1915.

The Great Survey

The task of the Canadian Pacific Survey was immense: to identify a viable land route through the rock and muskeg of the Canadian Shield, across the vast, mostly unoccupied plains and, most daunting, through the Rockies and other mountain ranges of British Columbia to the Pacific Coast. Sandford Fleming logically divided the survey into three regions: the Woodland Division north of the Great Lakes, the Prairie Division and the Mountain Division. He had 800 men at work in 1873, the first survey season, increasing to more than 2,000 in subsequent seasons. The supply problems alone were monumental, as the survey crews were spread out over 3,000 miles of untamed country.

did he blaze trails for several major railways but he went on to devise our modern system of Standard Time and the division of the world into time zones; he conceived the Pacific Cable, linking countries of the British Empire telegraphically; and among numerous other accomplishments, he designed Canada's first postage stamp.

In 1872 Sandford Fleming personally covered the 5,300-mile distance across the continent from Halifax to the west coast. It was a historic expedition by a professional engineer intent on proving the possibility of an all-Canadian rail route from the Atlantic to the Pacific. Accompanying Fleming on this journey was George M. Grant, who kept detailed notes which he later incorporated into one of the most famous of early Canadian travel books, *Ocean to Ocean*. As a route through the Rockies, Fleming opted for the established, northern Yellowhead Pass, travelled by Alexander Mackenzie, Simon Fraser, the Overlanders and others. Grant later noted their satisfaction with the Yellowhead: "Instead of contracted canyon or savage torrent raging among beetling precipices as half feared, the Pass is really a pleasant open meadow. So easy an egress into the heart of the Rocky Mountains as that of the Jasper Valley, and so favourable a pass as the Yellowhead could hardly have been hoped for."

Fleming's preference was for a route from the Yellowhead westward via the North Thompson and Fraser Rivers to tidewater at Burrard Inlet, near the site of what is now Vancouver. However, he painstakingly examined half a dozen other possible passes through the Rockies, for there were many other points of view on this hotly debated topic. For example, Walter Moberly, Fleming's headstrong first engineer who was placed in charge of the survey in the Mountain Division, was in favour of a more southerly route through the Rockies. Moberly had explored the mountains and knew how challenging it would be to build a rail line through them; he wrote directly to the prime minister: "I don't know how many millions you have, but it is going to cost you money to get through those canyons." Given the complex geography of Canada's new Pacific province and the competing ambitions of emerging coastal communities to become the railway's terminus, perhaps it is not surprising that these issues remained a source of continuing controversy for another decade.

On his return, Fleming organized one of the greatest surveying projects ever undertaken in North America, if not the world.

Fleming's army of surveyors scoured the harsh western geography

40

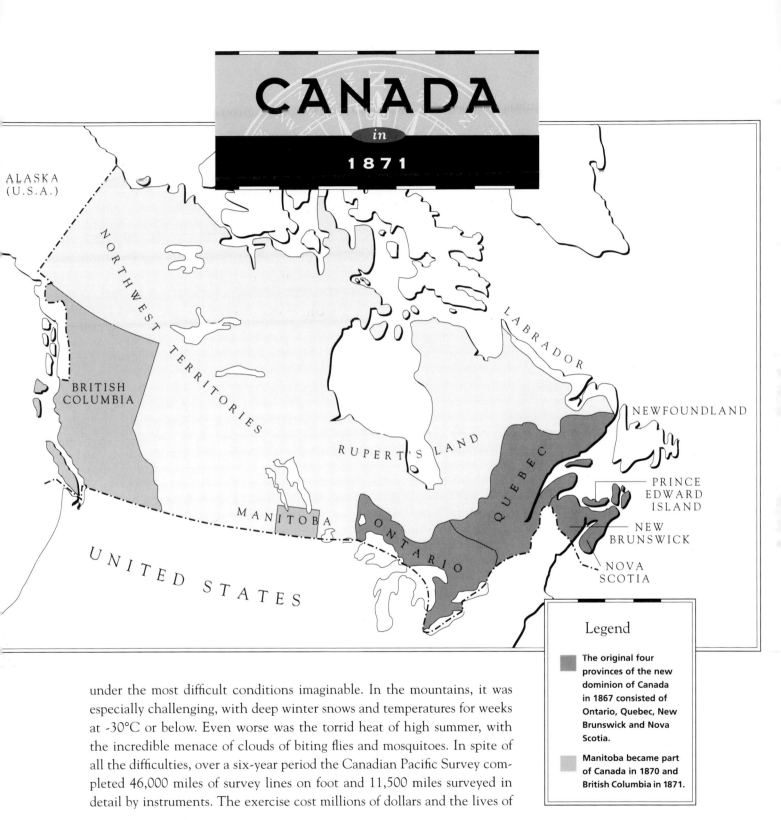

CANADA
in
1871

ALASKA
(U.S.A.)

NORTHWEST TERRITORIES

BRITISH COLUMBIA

LABRADOR

NEWFOUNDLAND

RUPERT'S LAND

MANITOBA

ONTARIO

QUEBEC

PRINCE EDWARD ISLAND

NEW BRUNSWICK

NOVA SCOTIA

UNITED STATES

Legend

The original four provinces of the new dominion of Canada in 1867 consisted of Ontario, Quebec, New Brunswick and Nova Scotia.

Manitoba became part of Canada in 1870 and British Columbia in 1871.

under the most difficult conditions imaginable. In the mountains, it was especially challenging, with deep winter snows and temperatures for weeks at -30°C or below. Even worse was the torrid heat of high summer, with the incredible menace of clouds of biting flies and mosquitoes. In spite of all the difficulties, over a six-year period the Canadian Pacific Survey completed 46,000 miles of survey lines on foot and 11,500 miles surveyed in detail by instruments. The exercise cost millions of dollars and the lives of thirty-eight men by drowning, forest fire, exposure and illness.

We know something of the harsh reality of life on a mountain survey team because of the detailed diary left behind by Robert Rylatt, a resolute Englishman hired by Walter Moberly to serve as agent in charge of supplies and equipment for a survey party in the Rockies. Rylatt left his ailing wife in Victoria and embarked on a two-year adventure in the mountains as a railroad pioneer. His many miseries included living and working through unending rainstorms:

> My drenched clothing is taken off at night, wrung out, and I turn into my equally wet blankets. When resuming my clothing in the morning, I shiver all over, and the teeth chatter, as I dolefully reflect how difficult it will be to prepare a meal. Imagine men like these; hard worked, forever wet, and poorly lodged, rising early on such mornings as we are experiencing, and instead of a warm solid breakfast, stand shivering and swallow slapjacks half baked, larded over probably with bacon grease, or maybe a rasher of Bacon, the appetite for such viands stimulated by a muddy compound honoured with the cognomen of Coffee, the beans probably being placed in a piece of canvas, and bruised between two rocks, and when dished out having neither the aroma nor flavour of that refreshing beverage.

Rylatt's survey party consisted of four officers (surveyors), sixteen men—half of them Canadians—who served as axemen, plus eight Indian and Mexican packers and one Bavarian hunter. There were forty-five animals in the pack train, each carrying about 300 pounds. During summer months, good weather was not always a blessing, as the curse of mosquitoes sometimes made evenings unbearable:

> Tonight the misquitoes [sic] fairly drove me to bed supperless, they got into my eyes and nostrils; and when I opened my mouth to bestow my blessing, they were hurrying down my throat to meet it. Seizing my water can and a crust of bread, I made a shoot into my wigwam; Ah, but they are nimble on the wing, a cloud of the little wretches followed me in, and as I closed my curtain they had their insinuating little needles drove home, and were bleeding me merrily for supper.

But winter in the Rockies was the most fearsome. Indeed, it is a wonder that Rylatt and his survey party survived the deep snows and bitter cold they experienced during the Christmas season of 1871:

> Our Christmas day passed very quietly; the weather clear and cold, 34 below zero. On the following night (26th) the mercury became frozen; it was contained in a glass Ginger Beer bottle, and is used for the artificial horizon, and was, save a globule the size of a pea, frozen solid. Eating dinner, and more particularly Breakfast, was a matter of difficulty; the cook house was snugly built, and the cook kept up a roaring fire, and yet, the food served hot, would be frozen on our plates before we could consume it: all have to be well wrapped up when out in the air; force the breath from the mouth, and at the same instant strike the hand through it, and a slight resistance can be felt as it comes in contact with the frozen minute particles.

After enduring two full years of extreme conditions in the Rocky Mountains, suffering from scurvy, and having received the sad news that his wife back home had "passed beyond the stream of time," Rylatt received permission from Moberly to resign from the survey. However, the journey home in the company of a burly Scots companion was an epic adventure in itself, taking the entire spring season of 1873 to make their way back by foot to the coast. A full month into the journey home, tired and sick, Rylatt and his partner rested in a meadow about 150 miles out of Kamloops. The fatigued and weather-beaten men began "cogitating on the possibilities and probabilities of the Canadian Pacific Railroad" and fell into a kind of hallucinatory trance: "In the mind's eye we pictured a train of cars sweeping along over this flat, over the fierce streams we had passed, puffing and snorting up the mountains in gentle curves and windings, shrieking wildly as some denizen of the forest, scared at the strange monster . . . is hurrying off."

Their graphic fantasy included the looks in the eyes of the passengers on that imaginary train, the smell of the mouth-watering foods in the dining car, and the conversation of the passengers upon noticing them in the field: "Those two fellows yonder seem to have it pretty much to themselves . . . and are doubtless happier and more at freedom than we."

Rylatt's vision of passenger rail service was premature by a dozen years.

The Columbia Mountains

*B*etween Golden and
Revelstoke in British
Columbia lie the Columbia
Mountains, which consist of
four ranges: the Monashees,
Selkirks, Purcells and Cariboos.

The Columbia Mountains
originated as sediments
deposited 600 million years
ago. As the earth's plates
moved, heat and pressure
hardened the sediments into
hard rocks. These rocks
underwent several periods
of uplift into mountains,
followed by erosion and subsequent deposits. About 185
million years ago, the rocks
underwent their most recent
uplift to form the Columbia
Mountains of today.

The thick forests are home
to mountain goats, black and
grizzly bear, mule and white
tail deer, and moose.

The Canadian Pacific Survey, in which he played a small role, completed its work in a thorough manner. The actual construction of the railway, however, was a gargantuan challenge made even more complicated by the vicissitudes of both politics and finance.

Perhaps Prime Minister John A. Macdonald and his Conservative government were reckless in their enthusiasm for a transcontinental railway, but the drive required to build a great new nation demanded such passion. On two key points, Macdonald was firm: first, the railway would need to follow an all-Canadian route north of Lake Superior, rather than giving in to a path of least resistance by linking up with already-established American rail lines through the west; second, a private company should take on the task of building the national dream. The Intercolonial Railway connecting central Canada with the Atlantic region had been built as a government work, but the lessons of that commitment persuaded the Macdonald administration that the Pacific railway might bankrupt the young country. At least part of the enormous burden of this new national enterprise would have to be undertaken privately. It was also obvious that Canadians could not supply the necessary capital themselves. Somehow, large amounts of foreign capital would have to be raised, while at the same time ensuring the railway remained in Canadian control and served genuine Canadian interests.

In its effort to persuade a private firm to undertake the great project, the government was prepared to provide cash subsidies and generous land grants. Eastern Canada's largest railway company, the Grand Trunk, immediately ruled itself out because of Macdonald's stubborn insistence on locating the line north of the Great Lakes, arguing that such a route would be almost impossible to build and unprofitable to operate. The Grand Trunk's lack of interest revealed the dilemma of Canada's transcontinental railway strategy, as dreams of nationhood ran into calculations of real dollars and common sense.

A proposition was made to the government by Hugh Allan, the Montréal steamship magnate, said to be the richest man in Canada at the time. Somewhat unsettling, however, was the fact that Allan's financial backers and potential partners were Americans. Another group came forward from Toronto, the Interoceanic Railway Company. Bitter private and public disputes between the two companies prompted the government to intervene, forcing them to merge and allowing Hugh Allan to become president of

KAMLOOPS TO BANFF
East of Rogers Pass, the town of Golden, B.C., on the Columbia River with the Purcell Mountains in the background.
Doug Leighton

the new Canadian Pacific Railway Company, with the requirement that he dissociate himself from his American business connections. Early in 1873 the company was chartered by Parliament to take on the grand task.

Allan proved to be a very poor choice to lead the new enterprise. Not only was he ineffective in raising capital for the railway in England but he secretly continued to cultivate his former American partners. Far more serious, in that era of buccaneer business, Allan thought nothing of bribing politicians to further his railway ambitions. In the intense world of Canadian partisan politics, it was revealed that he had supported the Conservative party in the 1872 election with more than $350,000 in campaign funds, the equivalent of several million dollars today. For this cash contribution, he had apparently extracted a promise that he would become president of the Canadian Pacific Railway Company. This was the famous Pacific Scandal that led to the downfall of the Macdonald government. During the investigation and exposé of details of the scandal, the prime minister was surprised to see reprinted in the press a number of his telegrams sent to Allan during the final days of the election campaign, including the infamous plea: "Immediate, private, I must have another ten thousand. Will be the last time of calling. Do not fail me. Answer today."

The collapse of the government over the Pacific Scandal also caused the end of the Canadian Pacific Railway Company. It seemed as if the first great effort at western railway expansion had ended in failure. But the Canadian Pacific Survey continued its work as a new Liberal administration led by Alexander Mackenzie was voted into office in 1874. Mackenzie was an honest, hard-working prime minister, lacking the large, nation-building aspirations of his predecessor. When the terms of union with British Columbia were signed in 1871, Mackenzie had angrily denounced them, declaring that the agreement was "a bargain meant to be broken." Now, as he and his Liberal colleagues formed the government, the whole western world was settling down into what proved to be a prolonged and serious economic slump.

The depression made it doubly difficult to imagine anyone coming forward to finance a new transcontinental railroad. Unable to attract a commercial interest to take up the challenge, the government decided to undertake the railway as a public work. However, it would not commit to its completion under the terms of union with British Columbia, which strained relations between the federal government and the Pacific province to the breaking point. Talk of secession was heard in British Columbia; many wondered if union with the United States would have made more sense than joining Canada after all. A "Fight Ottawa" stance was assumed by politicians in Canada's westernmost province, a theme that has persisted until the present day.

In spite of economic difficulties, political squabbling and a general absence of the vision that had inspired the dream of a transcontinental nation, the railway did make progress under Mackenzie. The great survey of the rail route was completed and construction was commenced in a piecemeal, provisional fashion, beginning with improvements to the link between Ontario and Manitoba. The Yellowhead Pass was selected as the preferred route through the Rockies, and the Fraser River to Burrard Inlet passage was chosen as the crucial route to the west coast.

This cautious, painstaking approach was swept aside, however, when John A. Macdonald staged a surprising comeback by winning the next general election in 1878. "The Old Chieftain," as Macdonald was called by his Tory supporters, campaigned on a platform of the National Policy a key element of which was the quick completion of the transcontinental railway. With the conduct of the Conservatives in the Pacific Scandal forgiven or forgotten, the country returned to the original railway policy that once had held so much promise but failed disastrously. Fortunately, the economy was now strengthening and new options were emerging. The government awarded a contract in 1879 for the construction of the first 100 miles of track west from Winnipeg. Contracts were also signed with Andrew Onderdonk, an American engineer, to construct the extremely challenging rail line between Yale and Kamloops in British Columbia, through the rugged Fraser and Thompson canyons.

The Macdonald government also returned to its previous goal of finding a suitable group of Canadian capitalists to take on the massive railway project. This time, after extended negotiations, a Canadian syndicate with western railway experience was chosen to take on the formidable task. The syndicate was represented by George Stephen, president of the Bank of Montreal, and his cousin Donald Smith, who had served as chief commissioner of the Hudson's Bay Company. Both were Scotsmen, and they complemented each other with Stephen's eastern financial savvy and Smith's intimate knowledge of the northwest. They had joined forces with James Hill, a Canadian who would go on to become one of the greatest

Major A. B. (Hell's Bells!) Rogers, the determined American surveyor who in 1882 discovered Rogers Pass.
Whyte Museum of the Canadian Rockies
V547 PA12-18

American railroad builders of all time. Together, they had scored a dramatic success by acquiring a bankrupt Minnesota railway, the St. Paul, Minneapolis and Manitoba, and in short order building it into a flourishing enterprise. The reorganized rail line, which connected across the border to Manitoba, became one of the most profitable railways in America, and the principals became fabulously wealthy. "Catch them before they invest their profits," a cabinet minister is said to have advised John A. Macdonald. And he did.

The group agreed to build the great Canadian railway for a cash subsidy of $25 million and a land grant of 25 million acres. With the revived name of "Canadian Pacific Railway," the company would also have surrendered to it all of the government-constructed rail lines. In addition, the new railway was given extensive tax and customs concessions and was protected for twenty years from any competition south of its main line and connecting to American railroads. In turn, the company pledged to complete the railway within a decade and to equip and operate it "efficiently" and "forever." Despite criticisms of the deal and suggestions that the government was giving away far more than was necessary, Prime Minister Macdonald believed it was a good agreement and was exceedingly anxious to see the rail line completed. On February 16, 1881 the Canadian Pacific Railway (CPR) was incorporated and shortly thereafter began operation and construction westward.

George Stephen resigned his presidency at the Bank of Montreal in order to take on the chief executive position at the CPR. While Stephen provided the financial acumen necessary to see the project through to completion, James Hill provided the ruthlessness. Hill's first decision was to reject the route west of Winnipeg selected earlier by Sandford Fleming, arguing that the northern Yellowhead Pass would take longer and cross too many river valleys. The advantages of a shorter southern route seemed obvious, except that no one was certain that an acceptable pass through the Rockies could be found. Certainly the Canadian Pacific Survey had not identified an ideal southern route through the mountainous curtain. Shortly after incorporation, Hill dispatched Major A. B. Rogers, an American railway survey engineer, to search for a more southerly pass through the Rockies and the Selkirks. Among the inducements offered to Rogers was a cash bonus of $5,000 if he was successful and the promise that the pass would be named after him.

Opposite page:
KAMLOOPS TO BANFF
On the Kicking Horse River,
the town of Field, B.C., in
Yoho National Park.
Doug Leighton

The energetic William
Cornelius Van Horne,
the American who worked
for the CPR and helped
Canada to realize its
national dream of a
transcontinental railway.
B.C. Archives and Records
Service 39461 B6638

A pioneer work locomotive
nicknamed "Old Curly"
in the Canadian Pacific
Railway's Pacific Division.
Kamloops Museum and
Archives 607

A mythic figure, "Hell's Bells" Rogers was a wiry wisp of a man, known for his intimidating, offensive language and an ability to survive in the bush for days on end with few rations or supplies. He scoured the western mountains for a year and a half before finally locating the route that the railway today follows. Rogers determined that the Kicking Horse Pass would offer a difficult but viable route through the Rockies to the Selkirks where, in the summer of 1882, he discovered the pass that now bears his name.

During the CPR's first year of operation, the pace of western construction matched neither hopes nor expectations. Hill now recruited another American to oversee the entire project: William C. Van Horne. This proved to be one of the most important decisions made in the history of the railway. Van Horne had extensive experience managing midwestern American railways, and he was a man of great organizing abilities. From the moment he assumed the position of general manager of the CPR, the construction project assumed a surprising focus and a relentless drive. Indeed, the fantastic mobilization that occurred under the direction of this imported American often resembled a war effort or national emergency.

Van Horne took on the job in January of 1882 and immediately made the commitment to build an astonishing 500 miles of rail line that year in the direction of the western mountains. In spite of a late start caused by record flooding on the prairies, Van Horne soon had 5,000 men and 1,700 teams of horses in the field. He built accommodation trains for the workers and organized supply trains that each

Kicking Horse Pass

Kicking Horse Pass was discovered in 1858 by Dr. James Hector during an expedition commissioned by the British government to explore and map various portions of western Canada. The name came from the fact that at this spot Dr. Hector was kicked by one of his pack horses and knocked unconscious for several hours. Although in severe pain, he continued with the expedition.

Following pages:
KAMLOOPS TO BANFF
Wapta Lake in Yoho
National Park, near Field.
Doug Leighton

Members of the British Association for the Advancement of Science inspect a tunnel at Mount Stephen, September 1884.
Whyte Museum of the Canadian Rockies
V143 PA421-3 NA66-2292

carried a mile's worth of ties, rails and spikes. At the railhead, the ties were loaded on carts and distributed along the graded roadbed. In an era when everything relied upon manual labour, small armies of men carried the rails forward, waited for them to be properly positioned on the spaced ties and then proceeded while they were joined and spiked.

Van Horne pushed the steel rails forward at the rate of three miles per day, constructing more than 400 miles clear across Saskatchewan in that first season and adding 100 miles of branch lines in Manitoba in order to meet his target. During the following summer of 1883, the rail line was extended as far as Calgary and on to the Kicking Horse Pass.

The difficult route north of Lake Superior was being built simultaneously. James Hill argued strongly that this eastern portion of the rail line was an expensive mistake; he saw tremendous advantages in having the CPR follow a route south of the Great Lakes through American territory and linking up with U.S. railroads. This was one occasion, however, when he did not have his way. The government insisted on an all-Canadian route and would not waver. In frustration, Hill resigned from the CPR in May 1883, returning to the northwestern United States where he built his own railway empire. He left behind in his native country a legacy of key personnel and crucial decisions that would significantly shape the course of western Canada's development.

The mountain sections of the CPR involved unbelievable challenges. As the rail line edged into the Rockies from the east, constant rains, washouts and winter avalanches created havoc and seriously hampered construction. Meanwhile, from the west, Andrew Onderdonk was achieving the near-impossible as his legions of workers dynamited their way up the Fraser Canyon. A shortage of labour had prompted Onderdonk to import boatloads of Chinese "coolies." Some came from San Francisco, but most hailed from the Guangdong region of China. They came to British Columbia with the dream of earning enough money to return home wealthy. For Onderdonk, the more than 5,000 Chinese labourers he imported were more dependable than white workers, who also demanded higher wages.

Construction crews blasted tunnels through rock walls and carved roadbeds from the sheer cliffs of the Fraser and Thompson River canyons. Using the Cariboo Road, built during the gold rush, and small paddle wheelers, Onderdonk had supplies delivered to distribution points along the route. To facilitate the transportation of rails and other heavy supplies, he built a rail line through the lower Fraser Valley to the initial Pacific terminus at Port Moody. However, in the summer of 1884, Van Horne visited the coast and, to the surprise and grave disappointment of real estate developers and speculators, decided to move the CPR's terminus farther west to the site of what is now Vancouver. In fact, Van Horne and the railway decided the location, sites and names of major cities like Vancouver as well as smaller communities throughout western Canada.

So eager was Andrew Onderdonk to complete his construction contract through British Columbia's wild geography that he had a special 127-foot steamer built to speed up the delivery of supplies above Hell's Gate in the Fraser Canyon. But to get there, the SS *Skuzzy* first had to nav-

A portrait of Andrew Onderdonk, the American contractor who built the CPR line through the challenging Fraser Canyon section.
B.C. Archives and Records Service 2917 A1321

The SS *Skuzzy*, which Andrew Onderdonk managed to get through Hell's Gate in 1882 to provide paddlewheeler transport for supplies in the upper Fraser Canyon.
Vancouver Public Library 390

Glenbow Archives NA789-43

Opposite page:
KAMLOOPS TO BANFF
East of Field is the land
through which the Spiral
Tunnels run. The Yoho
Valley is in the background.
Doug Leighton

igate upstream against the onrushing white waters of Hell's Gate itself. In the fall of 1882, as onlookers from afar came to witness the dangerous attempt to beat the rapids, wagers flowed, with the odds as high as one hundred to one against the *Skuzzy*. After days of fighting the river, it was clear that the steamer could not succeed on its own. Undeterred, Onderdonk had ring bolts driven into the rock walls of the canyon. Ropes were attached to the *Skuzzy* and passed through the ring bolts, enabling 165 workers and a steam winch to pull the boat upstream through the rapids. It was the only time a vessel of any kind successfully negotiated the rapids of Hell's Gate.

This was a playful if dangerous episode in the daunting task of moving the railroad towards completion. The project in the mountains required hundreds of tons of dynamite and engineering feats such as erecting a massive cantilever steel bridge which had been fabricated in Britain, shipped to the Pacific coast and carried by rail from tidewater to Cisco in the upper Fraser Canyon. Onderdonk completed his government contract in 1884 and was then hired by the CPR to continue his impressive work past Kamloops towards the Eagle Pass, where the rail line was to meet up with the crews grinding their way through the mountain ranges from the east.

The human cost of the dangerous work in the western mountains was both terrible and tragic. In the haste to complete the rail line, workers were caught in rock slides and crushed in collapsing tunnels. Some fell off bridges being constructed high above the Fraser and other treacherous rivers. The toll was particularly high among Chinese workers, many of whom died as a result of illnesses such as scurvy, the severe climate or from accidents caused by the careless handling of explosives. More than two hundred Chinese workers died during an epidemic at Port Moody in 1883. During Onderdonk's construction contracts, at least six hundred Chinese perished, a cost of four men for every mile of track. Many of the survivors returned to China with their earnings, but a number remained in Canada to raise families.

This great Canadian enterprise was, in truth, an international effort. Scotsmen like George Stephen and Donald Smith were certainly crucial to the railway, as were Americans like Major Rogers, Andrew Onderdonk and William Van Horne. The railway navvies were made up of Canadians as well as labourers from around the globe. European stone masons were brought in to construct specially designed railroad bridges. The Chinese

A rare photograph of some of the thousands of Chinese labourers who worked on railway construction in the interior of British Columbia.
Vancouver Public Library 1773

workers were indispensable to the goal of completing the rail line from the Pacific coast through British Columbia's interior canyons. And, often overlooked, is the contribution of the native Indians of western Canada. Contrary to the false historical image of awestruck Indian horsemen scampering away from the fire-belching Iron Horse, native workers from many of the bands in the Fraser and Thompson River regions were employed driving the first CPR grade and steel through the mountains.

All of these tremendous efforts would have been jeopardized but for the financial genius of George Stephen, who devised a plan which freed the railway from the heavy burden of fixed debt charges, assuring its ultimate success. In the short run, however, this strategy exposed the CPR to the hazards of hand-to-mouth financing. By early 1884, drastic measures were required. It was impossible to sell any more stock in the railway, and more than half the government subsidy remained to be earned. With his

own resources strained beyond limit and creditors yelping at his heels, Stephen turned in desperation to the government for assistance. He asked John A. Macdonald for a government loan of $22.5 million on the security of a first mortgage on the railway property. It was a tremendous amount which threatened to risk the national credit at a time of declining revenues. However, Macdonald could not bring himself to abandon his grand design, and his government was able to get the loan bill through Parliament.

So near and yet so far. Construction continued, but by the end of 1884, with the conclusion of the great project in sight, money ran out again. It was becoming politically impossible for the government to provide any further support, yet it looked as if the company would collapse, almost within view of its goal. Suddenly and unpredictably, fate intervened.

In the fall of 1884, Louis Riel had returned to Canada to assist the Metis and native people in their conflict with the Canadian government. Fifteen years earlier, his leadership of the Red River Rebellion had indirectly resulted in the promise of a railroad across the continent. In the spring of 1885 his sparking of the Northwest Rebellion provided a golden opportunity for the CPR to demonstrate how the railway could help preserve law and order in the west. Van Horne was able to quickly move military troops via rail to the northwest and, by the summer, the rebellion was quashed. Riel was tried, found guilty of treason and sentenced to hang. Later that year he was executed in prison in Regina.

It was suggested by some wags that the CPR should erect a monument to Louis Riel. The railway's key role in putting down the rebellion was ample justification for further government assistance, allowing construction to press on to a rapid conclusion. Onderdonk completed his line to Eagle Pass by the end of September 1885, but it took another six weeks for the crews from the east, who were building the line through remote mountain passes and almost impossible grades, to arrive at Craigellachie, the designated location for completion of the transcontinental rail line. Craigellachie was the name of a rallying point in Scotland for the Grant clan, from which both Donald Smith and CPR President George Stephen were descended. Craigellachie was a symbol of defiance. During one of the darkest hours of the great project, when the financial and political hurdles seemed far too overwhelming, Stephen sent a brief, cryptic telegram to his cousin, Donald Smith: "Stand fast, Craigellachie."

On November 7, 1885, in a simple ceremony at Eagle Pass in the Monashee Mountains, Donald Smith drove the railway's last spike. Following Van Horne's explicit instructions, there was no pageantry and no golden spike. Van Horne is reported to have said, "The last spike will be just as good an iron one as there is between Montreal and Vancouver, and anyone who wants to see it driven will have to pay full fare."

The small party of CPR officials and workers who were present cheered as the last spike was tapped into place. Called upon to make a speech, Van Horne's only words were: "All I can say is that the work has been done well in every way." It was an emotional moment for those assembled, including Major Rogers and Sandford Fleming, both of whom had played prominent roles in the railway saga.

Construction of the CPR had been completed across 2,000 miles of

Opposite page:
KAMLOOPS TO BANFF
The famous Moraine Lake in the Valley of the Ten Peaks near Lake Louise in Alberta.
Tim Thompson

The Last Spike

On Saturday, 7 November 1885, at 9:22 in the morning, at Craigellachie in the Rocky Mountains, Donald Smith was preparing to drive the last spike of the Canadian Pacific Railway. His first blow was a feeble one and the plain iron spike bent. A spare one was quickly set up and Smith hit this one with careful, precise blows, driving it into place.

There was a brief silence, followed by cheering and backslapping as the onlookers celebrated the completion of Canada's first transcontinental railway. The line was completed in just 54 months, almost six years ahead of schedule.

Today, a stone cairn marks the historic spot. The plaque on it reads: "Here was driven the last spike completing Canadian Pacific Railway from ocean to ocean November 7, 1885."

western frontier in five years, half the time allowed in the famous agreement. The Rocky Mountains had finally been conquered in an unparallelled feat of engineering and organization. This was an incredible achievement which at last made Canada a vertebrate nation, with the spine of a railway linking it from sea to sea. On that historic day, such thoughts and others must have been coursing through the minds of those witnessing the driving of the last spike at Craigellachie. Their thoughts would have been momentarily disturbed and focussed as never before by the sounding of the locomotive steam whistle and the satisfying call of the conductor: "All aboard for the Pacific!"

More than half a century later, with the benefit of hindsight, Canadian poet E. J. Pratt summed up the accomplishment of the completion of the transcontinental railway in his epic poem, "Towards the Last Spike." Pratt aptly wrote that "the stream of steel had found a way to climb, became a mountaineer" and in the process delivered the "smoky, lusty-screaming locomotives" to the Canadian Rockies.

A classic Canadian photograph: Donald Smith driving the Canadian Pacific Railway's famous last spike at Craigellachie, about 30 miles west of Revelstoke, 7 November 1885.
Glenbow Archives NA1494-5

An "end of steel" railway construction shanty town in Rogers Pass, 1886.
Whyte Museum of the Canadian Rockies
V701 LC226 NA66-950

Opposite page:
A Canadian Pacific Railway construction crew near Revelstoke, British Columbia.
B.C. Archives and Records Service H7010

The Transportation Revolution

The driving of the last spike marked the beginning of the railway age in western Canada. The completion of the country's first transcontinental rail line not only stimulated the rapid development and settlement of the west but also launched a romantic era of passenger travel. Soon there would be nothing more glamorous than taking a trip on the train, especially through the Rocky Mountains.

On June 28, 1886, the first transcontinental passenger train left Montréal for the Pacific coast, arriving at Port Moody 139 hours later on July 4. This was the historic "Pacific Express" consisting of a dining car, sleeping cars, and colonist, mail, express and baggage cars. Engines and cars were routinely dropped and changed en route, so that little of the actual train that departed Montréal arrived on the west coast.

Castle Mountain

At just over 8,950 feet, this bulky turreted peak is an excellent example of a castellate-type mountain (one that has horizontal rock layers). It was named for its obvious castlelike shape by explorer Dr. James Hector in 1858.

Opposite page:
**KAMLOOPS TO BANFF
Between Lake Louise and
Banff is Castle Mountain.**
Scott Rowed

A glimpse of the interior
of an early CPR dining car,
c. 1886.
Glenbow Archives NA3026-14

Top:

**The Canadian Pacific Railway's
first transcontinental train
crosses the Pitt River Bridge to
reach Port Moody, B.C., July 1886.**
Glenbow Archives NA4967-131

Within a few years, the luxurious "Imperial Limited" began making regular trips between Montréal and Vancouver, covering the distance in only four days. Considering that the same journey before the train had required a month of arduous travel, this represented a transportation revolution. The "Imperial Limited" featured observation cars with rooftop cupolas to allow passengers a panoramic view, pioneering the "dome car" concept that would become so popular by the middle of the twentieth century. The CPR also ran a special car with waist-high sidewalls for open-air touring during summer months in the Rockies.

None of this would have been possible, however, without the continual improvement and upgrading of the rail line. This was especially necessary in the early years of the CPR's operation, as the railway had been hurried through to completion. Ballast was added to the hastily built roadbed, ensuring more stability and a smoother ride. Massive wooden trestles, made of millions of board feet of lumber, were gradually replaced

by more permanent steel bridges. In 1893, for example, the 292-foot-high wood-frame Stoney Creek bridge, situated on the eastern approach to Rogers Pass and reputed to be the highest railway bridge in the world, was replaced by a steel-arch structure. Each improvement enabled the CPR to run heavier, more powerful locomotives.

Snow was the railway's biggest enemy. In fact, in the CPR's first few years of operation, extremely heavy snowfalls prevented year-round rail travel through the mountains. The route chosen by Major A. B. Rogers, particularly the pass that bears his name, is witness to some of the deepest recorded snowfalls in the world. Especially frightening were snow avalanches, roaring down the slopes without warning at speeds of 200 miles per hour, taking workers and heavy equipment with them.

The CPR established observation camps in the mountains to record the depth of snowfalls as well as the location and size of avalanches that covered the rail tracks. The dramatic reports from these winter camps resulted

Following pages:
KAMLOOPS TO BANFF
Morant's Curve beside
the Bow River in Banff
National Park.
Doug Leighton

Replacing the wooden Stoney Creek Bridge with an arch-shaped steel structure, c. 1893.
Glenbow Archives NA1459-52

An engine pulling a train across the Mountain Creek Bridge in the Selkirk Mountains. The original wooden bridge was 164 feet high, 1,1086 feet long and contained over 2 million board feet of lumber.
Glenbow Archives NA4140-30

Opposite page:
A train crossing the new steel Stoney Creek Bridge.
Glenbow Archives NA4680-11

in the decision to build over thirty huge snowsheds, constructed from massive timbers, to cover and protect the rail line through the Rogers Pass section. These structures had a combined length of over five miles and took two full construction seasons to complete. Special summer tracks were built outside the snowsheds in order to ensure that passengers were not denied the spectacular view of the Illecillewaet and Asulkan glaciers.

The need for safer winter and spring travel also prompted the CPR to make a number of dramatic improvements that resulted in its main line moving literally *through* the mountains rather than over them. In 1884, when railway construction crews came through the summit of the Kicking

The Stoney Creek Bridge

The Stoney Creek Bridge is located on the eastern slope of Mount Tupper. The bridge's design and beauty made it one of the world's most important in its time.

Originally, a wooden bridge spanned the canyon, but it was replaced in 1893 by an arched steel bridge that measured 336 feet in length.

By 1929, the weight of locomotives had almost doubled and the CPR was forced to replace the bridge again. Normally, new bridges were built beside existing ones, but because of the difficult terrain no other foundation could be used. As a result, the new bridge had to be built right over the old one, without placing any pressure on it. Today, the beautiful Stoney Creek Bridge spans 484 feet and towers 325 feet above the creek bed.

Horse Pass, they encountered a staggering drop, with no room in either the Kicking Horse Canyon or Yoho Valley to lengthen the line or reduce the gradient. On the western slope of the pass, the CPR won government approval for a very steep grade of 4.5 per cent—more than twice the maximum considered safe on a rail line. This was the famous Big Hill, permitted as a temporary measure so that construction of the railway's main line would not be delayed. The tracks were laid in an eight-mile-long breakneck descent from the top of the pass to Field, dropping 237.5 feet to the mile.

Considered the most hazardous stretch of track in Canada, the Big

VANCOUVER TO BANFF
**The Rocky Mountaineer train
running through colourful fall
foliage of aspen trees, west
of Banff, Alberta.**
Tim Thompson

Opposite page:
VANCOUVER TO BANFF
**The beautiful Vermilion Lakes
west of Banff, Alberta.**
Tim Thompson

Hill was said to make or break the men who took trains over it. Working in face-biting blizzards, with winter temperatures dropping to 30 and 40 below zero, crews were forced to contend with the nightmare of avalanches, rockslides, stalled locomotives and runaway trains. In order to haul a fifteen-car train up the Big Hill, four specially designed 154-ton engines were required: two in front and two "pushers" in the rear. Even then, wheels spinning on slippery tracks sometimes caused a train to stall; its steam whistle would echo through the mountains, calling for the assistance of another "pusher" to help get it over the crest of the hill. Some locomotives exploded under the stress.

An exterior view of snow-shed construction in the Selkirks, c. 1886. Note the massive timbers.
Glenbow Archives NA1753-21

An interior view of a snowshed under construction on the CPR line through the Selkirk Mountains, c. 1886.
Glenbow Archives NA387-21

A CPR "kicker" engine and crew at the summit of Rogers Pass.
B.C. Archives and Records Service 51726 C5211

Far left:
Getting up the Big Hill to the summit of the Rockies required a lot of steam power: here, two engines are pulling and two more engines are pushing a passenger train up the steep grade from Field, B.C.
B.C. Archives and Records Service 32327 B2949

Compared to the trip down, all of this was routine. At the top of the Big Hill, regardless of weather conditions, the brakeman got off and walked alongside the train, watching for signs of overheating brakes or skidding wheels. Switchmen waited at the safety switches; if the engineer's speed was the prescribed six miles per hour or less, he was allowed to continue down the hill. When a train went out of control, however, there was nothing to do but switch it onto one of three emergency spur lines where, as one old railroader put it, "wrecks could take place without hindering traffic on the main line."

Amazingly, in the quarter of a century that trains ran on the Big Hill, there was not a single accident involving a passenger train. But many labourers lost their lives on freight or construction trains. The very first work train down the hill after the line was completed ran away and plunged into the Kicking Horse River, killing three workers. An often-told story is the one about an engineer who lost a 40-ton snowplow, complete with crew, on the hill. On the way up from Field, his view was obscured by clouds of snow flying back against the window of his cab. It was not until he reached the top that he realized the plow was no longer in front of his engine. No one knew how a snowplow the size of a boxcar, with wings that cut a swath 16 feet wide, could break loose and leave the track without anybody noticing. A search party found it half-buried in the snow below the track; miraculously, the crew was still alive inside, badly shaken and clamouring to be dug out.

Another engineer won the dubious honour of riding a runaway engine all the way down the Big Hill. When his light engine lost control, he threw caution to the winds and made a joy ride of it, a reaction typical of the boisterous mountain division railroaders. Shouting to his terrified fireman, "Here goes for Field!" he signalled to the stunned switchmen that he wanted to stay on the main rail line. When he finally brought the engine to a halt at Field, he briefly enjoyed his celebrity as the only engineer to ride a runaway engine the length of the Big Hill. His glory, however, was short-lived; he was promptly fired by means of a telegram marked "Rush."

As traffic increased on the transcontinental railway, the CPR recognized that it was imperative to confront the engineering challenge of the Big Hill. The problem was solved in the early 1900s by adopting an ingenious tunnelling concept previously used in Europe. Two complete circles were tunnelled into the steep mountains on both sides of the Kicking

Banff National Park

Canada's first national park was established after a group of men tried unsuccessfully to register a claim to a naturally occurring hot springs in the Banff area. At the urging of Sir William Van Horne, president of the CPR, the Canadian government created a small reserve of 10 square miles named Rocky Mountain National Park in 1885. Two years later the park was extended to 250 square miles and named Banff National Park. Today, Banff National Park encompasses 2,456 square miles and contains at least twenty-five peaks which rise 9,800 feet ore more. It also has geological oddities such as hoodoos and mineral hot springs.

Opposite page:
Looking down the main street of Banff, Alberta, with Mount Rundle looming over it.
Tim Thompson

77

An early steam shovel on a CPR work train, used to help construct the line, c. 1890.
B.C. Archives and Records Service 61335 D1437

A construction camp at No. 1 snowshed on the CPR line.
Kamloops Museum and Archives 1308

A CPR construction crew in the interior of British Columbia, c. 1892.
B.C. Archives and Records Service 74862 G5584

The Spiral Tunnels

The geometry of the Spiral Tunnels is complicated. The track carves a 250-degree turn through the upper tunnel, then executes a 230-degree loop through the lower tunnel. In each case, the track actually crosses over itself, emerging from the mountain more than 50 feet lower than its entrance. With a long freight train, as the engine exits from the bottom portal of the lower tunnel, its tail end can be seen rattling overhead, entering the upper portal. Together, the two tunnels form a figure-eight, and they tend to disorient passengers with even the keenest sense of direction.

Horse River. This was a gigantic project which entailed drilling through crystallized limestone under the most difficult conditions. Two years, a thousand workers and almost 800 tons of dynamite were required to complete construction of the Spiral Tunnels. When opened to traffic in the summer of 1909, they were hailed as one of the engineering marvels of the world. They increased the length of the CPR main line by a distance of almost five miles but reduced the grade by more than half.

To the west, in the Selkirk Mountains, frequent avalanches in Rogers Pass continued to make the rail line dangerous and expensive to keep open, despite the protection of snowsheds. In the spring of 1910 a tragic series of slides resulted in sixty men being killed. This was followed by two more seasons of extreme avalanche danger. The CPR was forced to implement a radical change with the construction of the five-mile-long Connaught Tunnel under Mount Macdonald, completely eliminating a section of the main line over Rogers Pass. The double-tracked tunnel was completed in December 1916 after three years of work.

A century after the construction of the original CPR main line, major construction projects were still being undertaken to allow more trains to pass through the mountains at lower grades. The best example of this is the Mount Macdonald Tunnel, which was completed in 1988. At a cost of $500 million, it employed over a thousand workers and took four-and-a-half years to build. The tunnel is almost nine miles long, making it the longest railway tunnel in the western hemisphere. It passes more than 360 feet below the Connaught Tunnel and almost 1,200 feet below the summit of Rogers Pass. Near the centre of the tunnel, a sophisticated ventilation system based upon two vertical air shafts rises almost as high as the Empire State Building to the summit. The Macdonald Tunnel allows the CPR to move twenty-four freight trains a day through the pass, rather than the previous maximum of fifteen. "The Rocky Mountaineer" train continues to use the Connaught Tunnel in order to allow viewing of some of the scenic mountain vistas of the famous Rogers Pass route.

These constant and expensive improvements to the rail line through the mountains reveal the essential features of a railway: as a business, it is necessary to run safely, regularly and efficiently. Indeed, railroad economics are different from those of other businesses such as manufacturing. When you own or operate a factory or mill, for instance, if demand for your product declines, you can slow or halt production. Railways, however, which are very capital-intensive businesses, must run and keep to a schedule. As a result, it was almost always in the best interests of pioneering railways to promote industry and tourism, both of which generated the necessary traffic to earn a profit.

The CPR recognized this, and right from the beginning of operations it promoted travel in the Canadian west. Much of the effort to develop the railway as a first-class travel adventure with the highest quality of service can be credited to William Van Horne, who became president of the railway in 1888 and served in that position for more than a decade. The tough but respected American, described as "the ablest railway general in the world," became a Canadian citizen and in 1894 was knighted by Queen Victoria.

Sir William Van Horne loved the Rocky Mountains and, recognizing what a unique and powerful attraction they represented for travellers from around the globe, he sought to build the CPR's passenger service on the basis of their magical lure. Perhaps his most frequently quoted statement from this era is: "If we can't export the scenery, we'll import the tourists." It was largely as a result of his determined efforts and lobbying that Banff, Yoho and Glacier National Parks were established in the mid-1880s.

The genesis of the CPR's famous mountain hotels, however, has as strong a connection to the logistics of operating a railway under very challenging frontier conditions as any vision of developing tourism. In order to save the cost of hauling heavy dining cars up and down the steep grades of the Kicking Horse and Rogers Passes in the early years, Mount Stephen House was constructed at Field in 1886 and Glacier House was built at Rogers Pass a year later. Passengers could step off the train and enjoy fine dining in the midst of a glorious mountain landscape which a few years earlier had been largely uninhabited. This unparallelled travel experience became so popular that Van Horne quickly expanded facilities to allow for overnight accommodation as well. Thus, the railway found itself in the hotel business. Hotels were opened in Vancouver and Banff in 1887, with Van Horne personally selecting the site for the famous Banff Springs Hotel. The first chalet hotel at Lake Louise was opened in 1890. Complementing the construction of these world-renowned "castles in the wilderness," the CPR also launched a great Canadian tradition of grand railway hotels in major cities across the country.

In addition to promoting travel and accommodation in the "Alps of

Elk

Elk are large members of the deer family. They are dark brown in colour, with a large round tawny-coloured rump patch and a short tail. The average male weighs 660 to 990 pounds and stands 5 feet tall at the shoulder; the female is smaller. A male elk is easily recognized by its massive branching antlers.

Nearing the end of construction on the 5-mile-long Connaught Tunnel through Mount Macdonald, 1916.

Glenbow Archives NA1263-36

North America," the railway branched out with new lines throughout western Canada. By mid-1897 the CPR had received government approval to build a new rail line across the Rockies south of the Kicking Horse Pass, close to the American border. As a direct result of building a new railroad through the Crowsnest Pass, a significant coal-mining industry developed in the southern mountains of British Columbia and Alberta. This is merely one of many examples of the railway opening up a region for industrial development and directly benefiting from the increased freight and passenger traffic which followed.

As early as 1886 Canadian Pacific had chartered its first ocean-going steamships between Vancouver and the Orient. Within five years, the company's own Empress steamships were providing a regular service across the Pacific. Before the end of the century, Canadian Pacific Empress ships were carrying 60 per cent of all international first-class passenger traffic, with Canada's transcontinental railway providing connections for both Atlantic and Pacific ocean travel. The company successfully promoted itself as the "World's Greatest Travel System."

However, the CPR did not restrict itself to the travel and transportation business. From the beginning, it assumed the role of a national communications system, operating a network of telegraph facilities which followed the rail line and a national parcel express service. The company also played an important role in real estate development, immigration and settlement in western Canada, helping to establish the agricultural and grain industries on the prairies, which became known as "the breadbasket of the world."

The story is told about a traveller in the early years of the twentieth century who came to Canada to investigate investment opportunities. After crossing the Atlantic Ocean on a Canadian Pacific steamship, travelling to Montréal on a CPR train and registering at a grand railway hotel, he visited the company's Windsor Station headquarters to meet with CPR officials about conditions in western Canada. His questions answered, he went downstairs to the CPR ticket office to send off some telegrams by Canadian Pacific Telegraphs and some gift parcels via Canadian Pacific Express, as well as to purchase his rail tickets for travel onward to the

The CPR main line near
Mission, B.C., in the Fraser
Valley, during the flood
of 1894.
B.C. Archives and Records
Service 61383 F8648

Previous pages:
**The Rundle Range
near Banff.**
Scott Rowed

west. "There you are, sir," said the ticket agent, handing him an envelope full of tickets and reservation forms, "your train leaves tonight at eight o'clock." Since the city was then on daylight saving time, the agent added: "That's standard—railway—time."

"Good God!" exclaimed the traveller. "Does the CPR control the time too?"

This well-worn anecdote illustrates the comprehensiveness of Canadian Pacific's public services. The CPR was the first really big, modern corporation in the country. Especially in the west, it dominated the economic life of new provinces—like Alberta and Saskatchewan, created in 1905—and new cities, designed initially to service the railroad. During the construction of the CPR, crude, makeshift towns had emerged at the "end of steel." These were often temporary supply bases comprised of shacks and tents surrounding a few seedy saloons and hotels where workers were too easily parted with their wages. These primitive frontier settlements became part of the boom-and-bust pattern of railway development—for when the rails moved on, these "end of steel" communities often quickly became ghost towns. In contrast, divisional points along the rail line became important supply centres for crews servicing the railroad, giving rise to stable towns like Field, Revelstoke and Boston Bar. Of course, the railway also contributed to and shaped development in major cities like Vancouver and Calgary, where train stations and railway hotels dominated social and economic life.

In the 1880s, critics had complained that a transcontinental railway through empty terri-

A work camp on the Canadian Pacific Railway line near Golden, British Columbia, 1905.
Glenbow Archives NA780-1

The Canadian Pacific Railway depot on Burrard Inlet in Vancouver, c. 1890.
Glenbow Archives NA3688-14

tory would never generate enough revenue to pay for its axle grease. The CPR proved them wrong, of course, and by the turn of the century Canadians were calling for ever more railways; it seemed that the appetite for new railroads was insatiable. A twentieth-century construction boom resulted in Canada being able to boast of more miles of railway per capita than any other country in the world. Although a young country with a population of only six million, Canada soon had a mile of railroad for every 185 people, compared with a mile for every 400 in the United States and every 2,000 in Great Britain. This was because in the first fifteen years of the twentieth century, the total mileage of Canadian railways almost doubled, from 17,657 to 34,882.

Today, two great national rail networks weave their way through the Canadian Rockies; the CPR's competitor is the Canadian National Railways (CNR) system, owned by the federal government. The CNR story is dramatically different from that of the first transcontinental rail line and reveals the folly inherent in developing railways too rapidly in the optimism of a growing frontier.

Once the CPR had clearly established itself as a successful enterprise, there were actually two firms vying for the privilege of building the additional transcontinental railway that was apparently needed. Canada's economy was booming in the first decade of the new century and settlers were flooding into the west in unprecedented numbers. The headiness of these years might in part explain why the Liberal government of Wilfrid Laurier went so far as to grant separate charters to the Canadian Northern Railway and the Grand Trunk Pacific, both of which would complete rail lines to the west coast by the time of World War I.

The Canadian Northern was the brainchild of two westerners, William Mackenzie and Donald Mann, who had met each other while carrying out construction contracts for the CPR in Kicking Horse Pass. The two men were rough-and-tumble railway speculators destined to become tycoons by virtue of their reckless enthusiasm and entrepreneurial spirits. From a shoestring start in Manitoba, the Canadian Northern emerged as a major railway on the northern prairies, providing service to communities where the CPR did not run. It was a hodgepodge of small rail lines assembled and tied together by the remarkable derring-do of Mackenzie and Mann. Construction costs were kept to a minimum, rolling stock was obtained secondhand and traffic schedules were improvised.

Opposite page:
Two sure-footed mountain goats (*Oreamnos americanus*) at home in the Rockies.
Scott Rowed

Yellowhead Pass

To the west of the Athabasca and Miette Rivers is a broad, easily traversed pass through the Rocky Mountains. Locally it was known as Leather Pass, because large quantities of moosehide were transported through it. In 1823, an Iroquois Indian named Pierre Hatsination, an employee of the Hudson's Bay Company, made his first crossing of the pass. As he had a slight blonde tint to his hair, he earned the French-language nickname Tête Jaune, which means "yellow head."

This pass was the route originally favoured by a CPR surveyor in the 1870s, but it was rejected in favour of the more southerly Kicking Horse Pass route. The Yellowhead Pass was later used by the Grand Trunk and the Canadian Northern, the two main predecessors of the Canadian National Railways.

During the early years of the new century, the Canadian Northern Railway continued its aggressive policy of acquiring new rail lines where paying business might be immediately expected and where construction was likely to be cheap. While operating standards were primitive, they were adequate for the generally low density of traffic, although it was said that the Canadian Northern's track "had a regrettable tendency to jump up and hit the trains from behind." Nevertheless, Mackenzie and Mann began dreaming of building their growing network of scattered rail lines into a major new transcontinental railway. Soon they embarked on surveys for a rail line through the Rocky Mountains. However, the Canadian Northern had competition from a well-established eastern railway, the Grand Trunk.

The antithesis of the seat-of-the-pants approach epitomized by Mackenzie and Mann, the Grand Trunk Railway was controlled and ultimately managed from London, England. As a result, risks were rarely taken and opportunities were often foregone. The success of the CPR, however, persuaded the directors of the Grand Trunk to try a different style. Emulating the first transcontinental, they recruited and hired an experienced American railwayman, Charles Melville Hays, who began work as general manager of the Grand Trunk Railway Company of Canada on January 1, 1896. From that day forward, life would never be the same at the stodgy old railway.

Hays introduced American management methods into the operations of the Grand Trunk, imposing a faster, more informal, approach. He spotted weak links in the railway's network and immediately strengthened them; he also reduced operating expenses by 10 per cent, pleasing shareholders and the board in London. Most important, Hays recognized that as an eastern-based railway the Grand Trunk was becoming ever more dependent upon traffic from the west. He therefore advocated an aggressive new policy of expansion to the Pacific, arguing that the CPR and now possibly the Canadian Northern would drive the Grand Trunk out of business unless quick action was taken. In 1903, Hays established a subsidiary, the Grand Trunk Pacific Railway, to complete a new rail line to the west coast.

Of course, none of this made any sense. The young country may have believed in Prime Minister Wilfrid Laurier's prediction that the twentieth century belonged to Canada, but few imagined that the fledgling nation was actually ready to support two more transcontinental rail lines. It would be far more practical for the Canadian Northern and Grand Trunk to merge their operations, forming a single new transcontinental railway. In fact, Laurier did suggest such an approach, but his government would not go so far as to coerce the two railways into joining forces, and the stubborn directors of the two companies refused to consider such a proposition. Hays, who became president of the Grand Trunk in 1909, attempted a hostile takeover of the Canadian Northern, but Mackenzie and Mann were determined not to sell out. Instead, the two rival companies began a long struggle for the honour of becoming Canada's second transcontinental railway. It was a vain, futile competition that would end in failure for all concerned.

Both railways decided to cross through the Rockies via the northern Yellowhead Pass, the route that Sandford Fleming had originally proposed for the CPR. The Canadian Northern started its British Columbia section from Port Mann, near the mouth of the Fraser River, and ran parallel to the CPR line up the Fraser Canyon as far as Kamloops. In the process, it was forced to replicate the amazing feats of construction of Andrew Onderdonk, while continually crossing the Fraser to stay on the opposite bank from the earlier rail line. At Kamloops, however, where the CPR continued east, the new railway turned northward, following the North Thompson River almost all the way to the Yellowhead Pass. The last spike in the Canadian Northern's line was driven on January 23, 1915, about 10 miles south of Ashcroft, B.C.

Construction through the Yellowhead Pass

A portion of the Grand Trunk Pacific Railway track near Jasper Lake, c. 1911.
Glenbow Archives NA915-21

Top:
Level grade construction on the Grand Trunk Pacific line near Jasper, Alberta, c. 1911.
Glenbow Archives NA915-15

Bighorn Sheep

Bighorn sheep are one of the best-known animals of the Canadian Rockies. They are light grayish-brown and are easily recognized by their massive curling horns. Both male and female sheep grow horns, but the horns of females are very thin and rarely exceed 4 inches in length.

Opposite page:
A pair of Rocky Mountain bighorn sheep (*Ovis canadensis*), one male (with the big curling horns) and the other female.
Doug Leighton

was difficult and crowded, for both the Canadian Northern and the Grand Trunk Pacific were simultaneously laying tracks beside each other. In fact, the two railways were so close together in some places that it looked like a double-track line was being installed. Once through the pass, however, Charles Hays routed his Grand Trunk Pacific line due west, toward his dream of a new Pacific terminus. This was another epic feat of railway construction through rugged, granite mountains, over steep ravines and across raging rivers to the new community of Prince Rupert on British Columbia's northern coast. As the North American port closest to Asia, Prince Rupert was intended to be the next coastal metropolis.

No expense was spared in the construction of the Grand Trunk Pacific, and extra care was taken to build a straight and level route through the western mountains. Additional costs sent Hays to London in the spring of 1912 to raise more capital for his visionary plan of a new railway empire. No one can be certain whether he would have changed the future course of western Canadian railway development, for he journeyed back to Canada in April 1912 aboard the SS *Titanic* and perished in that ship's terrible disaster at sea.

The last spike in the late Charles Hays's pioneering railway was hammered near Fort Fraser on April 7, 1914, and two days later the first westbound train on Grand Trunk Pacific tracks arrived in Prince Rupert from Winnipeg. However, his grandiose dreams for the new port of Prince Rupert were never realized. In fact, construction costs for both of the new transcontinental railways were far higher than expected. Moreover, with the advent of World War I, the supply of capital from abroad was stopped, and the Canadian government was forced to meet interest payments in accordance with guarantees granted to both companies. As traffic declined and the economic situation steadily worsened, a royal commission was appointed in 1916 to investigate the crisis in the country's railways. The commission's report recommended public ownership of the Canadian Northern, Grand Trunk and other lines, forming a new, amalgamated, national railway company.

This was the genesis of the Canadian National Railways (CNR) system. Born in crisis, and in large part the direct consequence of the improvident obsessions to build rival empires, the CNR became Canada's second transcontinental railway, destined to compete with the CPR for traffic in western Canada and through the Rocky Mountains. The integration of

A family of tourists enjoying the view from the rear observation deck of a CPR railcar in the Fraser Canyon, 1910.
Whyte Museum of the Canadian Rockies
V653 NA80-748

the Canadian Northern and the Grand Trunk rail lines, as well as the CNR's rationalization of railway services across the country, took a number of years to complete. But in the post-World War I era, the new publicly owned railway emerged as a worthy competitor for the CPR. The CNR built impressive train stations and large railway hotels in major Canadian cities and, emulating its great rival, expanded into other transportation and communication services as well.

During the boom years of the 1920s and through the very tough economic depression of the 1930s, both the CPR and the CNR consolidated their positions as national rail networks and transportation conglomerates. In western Canada, the railways serviced and helped develop natural resources. Freight trains moved grain, lumber, pulp and paper, coal, potash, sulphur, copper, petrochemicals—and a host of other industrial commodities. This was the business that ultimately justified the insanity of building these ribbons of steel through the Rockies. Hauling such cargo is how the railways earned their income.

Passenger traffic, which was so important during the early years of the railways, eventually decreased in volume and importance. By 1936, as Canada was slowly beginning to recover from the great depression, the two national railways were carrying about 20.5 million passengers annually. A combined fleet of 6,000 passenger train cars of various types served almost every city and town in Canada. By 1941, the railways carried 30 million passengers, and during World War II, passenger business peaked at more than 60 million.

Following the war, traffic quickly dropped again to the 30 million level and continued to fall.

The reasons for the decline in passenger rail travel in the post-World War II era are many and varied. The rise of the automobile and the growth of national highway networks were likely the most important factors. Air travel also replaced rail as a much faster and more convenient method of transportation for both domestic travellers and tourists. However, even as passenger service became relegated to the status of a pleasant by-product of late twentieth-century railway services, it also maintained a dedicated core of loyal users. In an age when historic steam locomotives gave way to modern diesel engines, many travellers remained passionate about journeying across the country by train. And the steel rails that were implanted into the frontier by earlier generations of pioneers continued to provide the best possible vantage point from which to sit back and revel in the unique vistas of Canada's western wilderness.

A hiker feeding a moose.
Whyte Museum of the
Canadian Rockies V469 1536

Top:
A new era began with the invention of the automobile: here, a car has just crossed a road bridge over the CPR line alongside the Kicking Horse River.
Whyte Museum of the
Canadian Rockies V263
NA71-1678

Tall Tales

The exploration, surveying, construction and operation of railways through the Rocky Mountains has generated an abundance of folk-lore. Most of it is true.

Although some of the commonly told stories are fantastic in nature and difficult to believe, it must be remembered that they reflect the reality of an exciting frontier when people and events often seemed larger than life.

For instance, there is the legend of Bill Miner, who in 1904 made history by staging Canada's first train robbery, at Silverdale in British Columbia. He and his accomplice got away with $1,000 in cash, $6,000 worth of gold dust and $50,000 in U.S. bonds. Less than two years later, Miner was captured by a posse after holding up another train 13 miles east of Kamloops. But due to a scheduling

Opposite page:
The historic Banff Springs Hotel, dwarfed by the majestic Rockies.
Tim Thompson

97

A portrait of Bill Miner, who committed the first train robbery in Canada in 1906, shortly after his capture.
Kamloops Museum and Archives 878

Yoho National Park

Yoho National Park covers 507 square miles and is full of glacial lakes and waterfalls. The name comes from a Cree Indian word meaning "awe." One of the world's most interesting and famous fossils beds, the Burgess Shale, is located here. It contains the remains of more than 120 marine species dating back 530 million years.

change, he and his gang robbed the wrong CPR train that time and ended up with a mere $15 and a handful of liver pills! The Canadian frontier was supposed to be more peaceful and orderly than the American wild west, but Bill Miner proved otherwise. Sentenced to life imprisonment at the New Westminster penitentiary, within a year he escaped and vanished from Canada to the United States, where he became known as "the master criminal of the American west."

Then there is the story of the stolen church. In 1899, when the CPR decided that Revelstoke would be the railway's new divisional point west of the Selkirk Mountains, it meant the end of the town of Donald. Residents moved their belongings, including their houses, down the tracks to Revelstoke. They also prepared to transfer their prominent Anglican church, with its 600-pound silver bell. But when the crew arrived to move the church, they found the building had disappeared, "lock, stock and belfry." And no one was talking. It took some time to find out that the church had been hauled on a flatcar to Golden and loaded on a barge so that it could be transported an additional 100 miles up the Columbia River to Windermere, where two of Donald's former residents, who shared a strong attachment to their church, ran a general store. Many years later, when the citizens of Windermere gathered at the church to pay their respects to one of the merchants, who had died at the age of seventy-four, it was noted that never before in the history of Christianity had a man received his last rites in a church which he was alleged to have stolen.

What follows is a selection of stories that offer insights into the life and times of railways in Canada's western mountains. They provide a sense of the courage, stamina, humour and horror of the trailblazers who helped shape the early years of train travel through the Rockies.

The Major's Bath

Major A. B. Rogers was the American railway surveyor who discovered the famous mountain pass that bears his name. He was well known for his violent temper and use of profane language: "Blue Jesus!" was one of his favourite expressions. In the early 1880s, when he was scouring the Rockies and Selkirk Mountains for a southern route for the CPR, his frequent companion was an experienced mountain guide, Tom Wilson, who later recalled this experience with the major.

It was a very hot day and the glaciers were pouring torrents into the streams. On reaching the creek we found it terribly swollen, and to make matters worse the current raced around numerous large boulders. All streams that run direct from glaciers begin to rise in the afternoon and subside in the early morning. Knowing this, I halted at the creek and suggested to the Major that it would be advisable to camp for the night and cross the stream when the water would be lower and less dangerous. He shot one of his famous "Blue _____" oaths at me. "Afraid of it are you? Want the old man to show you how to ford it?" It all happened in half a minute; he spurred his horse in, the current took its legs from under it, the Major disappeared in the foaming, silt-laden water, and the horse rolled downstream.

I grabbed a long pole and managed to push it towards the Major; and he seized it and I hauled him ashore. The horse struggled to its feet and climbed out a little way below us. Once ashore, the old man, for so I had begun to think of him, gave me a funny look. "Blue _____," he remarked, "Light a fire and then get that damned horse. Blue _____, it's cold!" Needless to say we camped there that night and crossed the stream next morning.

This incident gave Bath Creek its name. The Bow River flows through Bow Lakes and there deposits its glacial silt in the flood season. Bath Creek flows direct from Daly Glacier, therefore there are many times when the Bow, before its junction with Bath Creek, is running clear; then the latter pours its torrent of silty water into the larger stream and discolours it for miles downstream. Whenever this occurred the men of our gang would remark, "Hello, the old man's taking another bath," hence the name.

The intrepid Major A. B. Rogers, here surveying the site of Yoho National Park.
B.C. Archives and Records Service 1234 G6162

The Stoney Indians

The Stoney Indians were given their name by white people because of the method of cooking that they used, which was to boil food by dropping hot stones into it. They moved westward from the Lake of the Woods region of eastern Manitoba, fleeing the flood of settlers, and finally put down roots in the foothills and mountains at the edge of the prairies.

Opposite page:
**BANFF TO CALGARY
Exshaw, Alberta, on the
Bow River, just 56 miles
west of Calgary.**
Scott Rowed

Dr. Hector and the Kicking Horse

Even earlier, in 1858, Dr. James Hector discovered the Kicking Horse Pass. Many years later, Hector's companion, Peter Erasmus, told how the famous railway pass received its name through a story that also reveals details of the hardships of early explorers in the mountains. In addition, Erasmus recalls the developing relationship with native Indian guides such as Nimrod of the Stony people (at that time, Stoney was spelled Stony).

We had been travelling through the mountains for about two weeks; our progress was very slow as sometimes we had to retrace our steps because of some impassable obstruction in our way. The doctor wanted to cross over to the Columbia River and to establish the latitude and longitude of the divide, going by compass as much as possible and only consulting the guide as a last resort.

Our food was getting low; Nimrod could find no game to replenish our dwindling supplies. Finally we were on short rations and gave up compass-reading for Nimrod's guidance north to where he promised better hunting.

We were following along a river bank as the easiest way in the direction we wanted to go when one of the horse's packs came loose. The horse lost his balance and tumbled backward into the river. The clumsy brute had been giving us trouble all the way. The river was quite deep and the banks steep. We all left our saddle-horses and rushed down to save the brute. Losing the pack would have been quite serious in our present situation as it contained most of our food supplies. Sutherland, an old cow puncher, roped the horse and we were able to finally get him on safe ground.

The doctor went to pick up his own horse which was feeding among some spruce with his lines trailing. The instant the doctor reached for the lines, the horse whirled and kicked him with both feet in the chest. The doctor was knocked unconscious . . .

Dr. Hector must have been unconscious for at least two hours when Sutherland yelled for us to come up; he was now conscious but in great pain. He asked for his kit and directed me to prepare some medicine that would ease the pain . . . I asked and got permission to try to find something to shoot. The accident happened in the early forenoon, and it was late in the afternoon before I got started.

I found some fresh deer tracks shortly after I left camp, but was too anxious, and startled them before I could get a good shot. Following them

A portrait of Dr. James Hector, who discovered Kicking Horse Pass in 1858.
B.C. Archives and Records Service 40338 B6979

I had another running shot, drew blood, but did not knock the buck down. I kept after the wounded deer, and before I realized that I had gone so far, it was dark, and I had lost my directions. It was hopeless to try to find the way in the dark so I built a fire and tried to forget that I was hungry, cold, and worried over the doctor. Nights in the mountains get pretty cold and that one was the longest and most miserable of any time I ever spent on the trail.

Early next morning I climbed a high place and got my directions from the fog rising from the river . . . Nimrod had gone on the hunt long before I got back empty-handed and tired to the party. The doctor was still in pain but feeling much better, for which I was thankful . . .

Late that evening our hunter hobbled into camp, empty-handed. He had fallen when he missed his footing while stalking some sheep. The doctor said he had a badly sprained ankle. It was already swollen, and looked bad. The doctor gave me instructions to treat the man's ankle, and then said, "Now, Peter, it's entirely up to you; that man cannot walk for a few days."

Nimrod gave me directions to where he had last tracked the sheep. I had not yet reached the place when I spotted some of the animals across a deep ravine. They had not seen me or scented my presence. Taking advantage of every cover I could, crawling on my knees for the most part, I reached a point directly opposite. Trembling with excitement and weakness, I slowly raised my head above cover and looked. There in plain sight was a big sentinel sheep, his head raised watching something in the opposite direction. He was standing dead still. I slowly pushed my gun across a dead log and tried to take aim, but my eyes watered and the gun shook so I had to wait to calm my nerves.

Biting my lips in vexation at my foolish nerves, I finally got a grip on myself, took aim, and fired. He gave a tremendous leap and landed twenty feet below, tumbling and rolling to the bottom of the ravine. I knew the sheep would be dead. The others disappeared in a twinkling of an eye. I lay for a moment stunned at the effectiveness of my long shot, then with a yell that echoed back from the mountain, scrambled and slid down the slope after my kill.

It was hard to keep from dancing and holding my gun in triumph as I had seen some of my Indian friends do after some extraordinary shot. I quickly skinned the animal, cut off a thigh for my carrying sack and hit

A Stoney Indian family,
Samson and Leah Beaver
with their daughter Frances
Louise, c. 1907. Samson
Beaver, like his predecessor
Nimrod, was also a guide.
Whyte Museum of the
Canadian Rockies V469 2771

back for camp, anxious to carry the good news to the others. Nimrod got up and hobbled over to where I had placed the meat. After examining the meat he turned to me in disappointment, "No good, Peter. No good. Can't eat." Then I remembered: I had killed a buck, and at that time of year, during the rutting season, they were not fit for human consumption.

My disappointment was the keener because of my early exultation over the kill. In my eagerness to get food I had completely forgotten one of the first lessons I learned from the Pigeon Lake Indians. This was the last straw, and I sat in silent misery . . .

The Stony did his best to prepare some of the meat but none of us could get it down. Sutherland kept on trying for trout; he gave a tremendous shout, finally landing one. One trout for six men was not a big meal but it helped a lot, especially with the Stony's herbs to add taste to the fish soup.

Nimrod, who knew of a salt lick only ten miles away where he would get a moose, also wanted to try again next morning, but the doctor ordered him to stay in camp. "Erasmus will go out again today, and tomorrow I will try to ride; we will go together to where you think you might get a moose. We'll ride within a mile of the place; maybe you can walk that far."

That morning, fortified with the rations of all three men and I suspect the doctor's share as well, I felt like a new man. I didn't see a thing all day, but on my way back to camp shot a partridge. I ate the gizzard raw and felt much better. It was a temptation to eat the rest of that small bird, but the thought of the men's sacrifice that morning was enough to overcome my greed.

The Stony immediately took charge of the bird for cooking, taking elaborate care that not a morsel would be wasted; he added his own mountain ingredients and apportioned the meat with the same care as he used in its preparation. "Drink the soup," he said, "it will do you more good than tea." The doctor took his share that night, the first nourishment since his accident. There was more cheerful talk that night than any of the last five nights, as we prepared to make an early start next morning.

Nimrod had been busy the previous evening preparing some kind of contraption that, he said, he would use the next morning on his moose hunt. He was humming a little song as he prepared to leave. I could see the contraption was to be a foot strap to take some of the weight off his foot. I rigged up a back strap for him to carry his gun and leave his hand free. "You know," said Brown, "that little beggar might just do what he says, kill a big moose, and he still can sing while the rest of us hate to talk; it takes too much energy."

We put the doctor on the quietest horse we had and started for Nimrod's promised land of the moose . . . after travelling about eight or nine miles, Nimrod mentioned that we had reached the place to stop . . . I watched him, curious to see how he managed that foot. Every time he put the lame foot forward, he pulled on the knee strap, giving him a kind of rolling motion. It worked, and he was still singing in a low tone hardly noticeable fifty yards away. Walking must have been painful, for his ankle was still black and swollen, yet he was cheerful and as determined as ever.

About four o'clock in the afternoon we heard a shot, then another. "Nimrod has shot a moose," I yelled. "Come on, let's go and find him."

"Go ahead," said the doctor. "If he has had any luck, we can move the camp later."

105

Moose

*T*he male moose is one of the largest antlered animals on earth, ranging in weight from 800 to 1,400 pounds, with an antler spread of 4 to 5 feet. The female moose is smaller and does not grow antlers. Moose are an overall dark brown/black colour and have a large upside-down bell-shaped sack which hangs from their bottom jaw.

It was tough going through the heavy brush and timber as we tried to go straight towards where we thought the sound came from. It sounded close but it was more than a mile before we got there. Brown followed close behind and when we saw our hunter, we both yelled together.

"What did you get, did you kill anything?"

"Moose, of course, moose," pointing with his pipe at the same time to where a big moose lay, close to the salt lick.

Smiling happily between puffs, he explained how he had nearly lost the moose when his foot sling had caught a stick and almost threw him into a pile of dry brush. The noise would have scared the moose, and it would have been out of sight before he could have gotten a shot. He had to wait a long time before the moose quieted down and he could approach to gun range.

We were proud of him, the smallest but the most courageous of us all. Brown walked up to him where he was sitting on a rock and said, "From now on, Nimrod, you're my brother. If my name was White instead of Brown, I'd give you my name, for I think you are the whitest friend any man could have."

When I interpreted Brown's long speech, Nimrod laughed and said, "I would rather be Red than White; it is closer to your colour than White, and tell him I am proud to be his friend, for he is more like my people than his own." Brown was a dark, swarthy man, with black hair and bristling black eyebrows. Brown got a big laugh out of my interpretation and shook the Stony's hand again.

Surveying in the Rockies for the "Glory of Glories"

In the 1870s, the Canadian Pacific Survey engaged an army of men under the most trying circumstances in a herculean effort to explore the challenging, largely unmapped geography of the western mountains. Chapter Two presented some of the details of Robert Rylatt's grim experience with a survey crew; a complementary tale of the tremendous trials and tribulations of these early mountain surveyors is offered by Pierre Berton in this excerpt from his 1970 book, The National Dream.

In the Thompson River country of central British Columbia, forty miles out of Kamloops, Roderick McLennan's survey party lost almost all of its pack animals in the winter of 1871. Eighty-six of them, McLennan reported to Fleming, died from cold, hunger or overwork.

An even worse winter expedition was the exploration launched in 1875 by E. W. Jarvis, who was charged with examining the Smoky River Pass in the Rockies. Fleming had already settled on the Yellow Head as the ideal pass for the railway, but this did not prevent him from carefully examining half a dozen others, just in case. Jarvis set off in January from Fort George with his assistant, C. F. Hanington, Alec Macdonald in charge of dog trains, six Indians and twenty dogs.

A CPR survey party at the summit of Kicking Horse Pass, November 1883.
Whyte Museum of the Canadian Rockies
V701 NA66-946

Both Jarvis and Hanington left graphic accounts of the ordeal, illuminated by uncanny episodes: the spectral figure of Macdonald knocking on the door of their shack in 49 below zero weather, sheathed in ice from head to toe; the lead dog who made a feeble effort to rise, gave one spasmodic wag of his tail and rolled over dead, his legs frozen stiff to the shoulders; and the auditory hallucinations experienced one night by the entire party—the distinct but ghostly sound of a tree being felled just two hundred yards away but no sign of snowshoes or axemanship the following morning.

The party travelled light with only two blankets per man and a single piece of light cotton sheeting for a tent. They moved through a land that had never been mapped. A good deal of the time they had no idea where they were. They camped out in temperatures that dropped to 53 below zero. They fell through thin ice and had to clamber out, soaked to the skin, their snowshoes still fastened to their feet. They stumbled down box canyons and found the way blocked by frozen waterfalls, two hundred feet high. They suffered from *mal de raquette*, a kind of seasickness brought on by the ups and downs of snowshoe travel. One day they experienced a formidable change of temperature—from 42 below zero to 40 above—and this produced a strange exhaustion, as if they were suddenly plunged into the tropics. One morning, while mushing down a frozen river, they turned a corner and saw an abyss yawning before them: the entire party, dogs and men, were perched on the ice ledge of a frozen waterfall, two hundred and ten feet high; the projection itself was no more than two feet thick. One evening they made camp below a blue glacier when, without warning, great chunks of it gave way; above them they beheld "masses of ice and rock chasing one another and leaping from point to point as if playing some weird, gigantic game." A chunk of limestone, ten feet thick, scudded past them, tearing a tunnel through the trees before it plunged into the river.

By this time it was March. Dogs were dying daily. Even the Indians were "in a mournful state of despair, declaring that they . . . would never see their homes again and weeping bitterly."

On March 15 Hanington described Jarvis as "very thin, very white and very much subdued." When they had reached the Smoky Pass, some time before, Jarvis had entertained grave doubts about proceeding further, but Hanington had said he would rather starve than turn back. It began to look as if he would:

The Chinese Workers

Andrew Onderdonk, who was contracted by the Canadian government to build the Fraser Canyon section of the rail line, began work in 1880 at Yale, B.C. He estimated that he needed 10,000 men to complete the task, but British Columbia's population was too small to meet his demands, so he imported Chinese workers from California. These men had railway experience, having worked on constructing the Union Pacific in the United States. Additional workers were brought in from China. The Chinese, who numbered more than 6,000 during this period, worked for a dollar a day.

"I have been thinking of 'the dearest spot on earth to me'—of our Mother and Father and all my brothers and sisters and friends—of the happy days at home—of all the good deeds I have left undone and all the bad ones committed. If ever our bones will be discovered, when and by whom. If our friends will mourn long for us or do as is often done, forget us as soon as possible. In short, I have been looking death in the face . . ."

Jarvis described "the curious sensation of numbness, which began to take hold of our limbs," as they pushed slowly forward on their snowshoes, giving the impression of men marking time in slow motion. Yet they made it. Hanington had lost 33 pounds; Jarvis was down to a bony 125. The food given them when they finally reached Edmonton produced spasms of dysentery and vomiting. Still they kept on, setting off once more across the blizzard-swept prairie for Fort Garry. All told, they spent 116 days on the trail, travelling 1,887 miles, 932 of those miles on snowshoes and 332 of them with all their goods on their backs, the dogs being dead.

Why did they do it? Why did any of them do it? Not for profit, certainly, there was little enough of that; not for adventure, there was too much of that. The answer seems clear from their actions and their words: each man did it for glory, spurred on by the slender but ever-present hope that someday his name would be enshrined on a mountain peak or a river or an inlet, or—glory of glories—would go into the history books as the one who had bested all others and located the route for the great railway.

The Dangers of Construction in the Fraser Canyon

During the 1880s, when Andrew Onderdonk built the CPR rail line along the seemingly impossible mountain walls of the Fraser Canyon, he did so by literally blasting his way through the rocky cliffs. Tons of explosives were used, often handled carelessly and revealing different attitudes towards life and death among the railway navvies. The terrible human cost of this mammoth construction project was described by Pierre Berton in his 1971 sequel to The National Dream, *entitled* The Last Spike.

All this time men were being mangled or killed by falling rock, by slides, by runaway horses, and above all by the incessant blasting that went on day and night. The temporary names along the way give a clue to the working conditions: "Jaws of Death Arch," for example, and "Indictment Hole," so named because, it was said, anyone who tried to put a right of

One of Andrew Onderdonk's construction crews at work on a tunnel in the Fraser Canyon section of the Canadian Pacific Railway.
B.C. Archives and Records Service H7008

way through the spot ought to be indicted.

Men grew careless with blasting powder and nitro-glycerine. At the ferry crossing at Spuzzum, tons of black powder were hauled to the edge of the bank by wagon and hurled down a chute into a waiting boat, the only cushion against the shock being a bale of hay. Some men whose hands were covered with blasting powder suffered severe burns when they recklessly tried to light their pipes. Others, returning prematurely to a half-finished tunnel following a blast, were met by a second, which blew them to pieces. One Chinese near Yale hid behind a tree two hundred feet from a tunnel about to be blasted and thought himself perfectly safe; a flying splinter sheared off his nose. Often, huge rocks came hurtling out of the mouths of tunnels like cannon-balls. One sank a boat, causing a man to drown. Another knocked down a bridge. The larger blasts touched off avalanches and mud slides. Almost every time heavy shots were fired inside a tunnel, great boulders were ripped free from the mountainside by the reverberations. One of these tore through the roof of the engine house at Number One Tunnel, "somewhat injuring a couple of men," in the casual report of the *Yale Inland Sentinel*. One slide came down from such a height that it carried part of an oak forest and an entire Indian burying ground into the river, allowing the oaks to continue to grow "and the dead men's bones to rest without being in the least disturbed—fences, roots, images and all." (The natives were more concerned about the "arbitrary

KAMLOOPS TO JASPER
Moose Lake at sunset, in
Mount Robson Provincial
Park, about 40 miles west
of Jasper.
Tourism B.C.

and illegal removal of the Indian dead" when the right of way happened to coincide with one of their cemeteries, but the railway builders paid little heed to such obstacles.)

Another rock slide actually blocked the Thompson River, forming a dam half a mile long and a hundred and fifty feet wide, raising the water two hundred feet and flooding several farms while leaving the channel below almost dry. The Chinese and Indians working in the vicinity dropped their tools and rushed to the river-bed to collect the hundreds of fish wriggling and gasping in the mud and also to recover the gold, which was still plentiful and, with the water down, easy to pan. Some made two hundred dollars a day in this manner until the river, working its way round the barrier of rock, formed a new channel. Another slide in November, 1882, blocked the track east of the Big Tunnel to a depth of sixty feet; it was mid-April before the debris could all be cleared away. An unexpected slide near Keefers station was struck by a train with such impact that the locomotive became detached. It hurtled over a 250-foot embankment, did a full somersault, and landed upright at the river's edge. The fireman and engineer climbed out, unhurt.

There was a curious accident at Cherry Creek caused by the near-desert conditions of the Interior Plateau of British Columbia. To one teamster hauling blasting powder by wagon, the rocks on the roadbed beneath suddenly seemed to take fire. The sight caused the horses to plunge forward, breaking loose from the wagon and pulling the driver, who held fast to the reins, right off his seat and away from the vehicle, which blew up with a roar. Later the mystery was unravelled: the dry weather had shrunk the staves of the powder barrels so that every seam leaked explosive. Thus both the floor of the wagon and the road beneath it were covered with loose powder, which was finally ignited by sparks made by the horses' shoes striking the rocks.

By Car and by Cowcatcher

Lady Agnes Macdonald, wife of Canada's prime minister Sir John A. Macdonald, in 1886 became the first person known to ride from Laggan (Lake Louise) to the coast on the cowcatcher at the front of a train. The railroad superintendent (Mr. E_____) was worried for her safety, but her husband (The Chief) relented, preferring the liquid refreshments of the lounge car for himself. Lady Macdonald later wrote about her experience, including the following description

114

of the trip through the Kicking Horse Pass and the giddy ride down the notorious Big Hill.

From Calgary to Laggan I had travelled in the car of the engine, accompanied by a victimized official. Perched on a little feather bench, well in front, and close to the small windows, I had enjoyed an excellent opportunity of seeing everything . . .

When I announced my desire to travel on the cowcatcher, Mr. E_____ seemed to think that a very bad job indeed. To a sensible, level-headed man as he is, such an innovation on all general rules of travelling decorum was no doubt very startling. He used many ineffectual persuasions to induce me to abandon the idea, and almost said I should not run so great a risk; but at last, being a man of few words, and seeing time was nearly up, he so far relented as to ask what I proposed using as a seat. Glancing round the station platform I beheld a small empty candle-box lying near, and at once declared that was "just the thing." Before Mr. E_____ could expostulate further, I had asked a brakeman to place the candle-box on the buffer-beam, and was on my way to the "Jamaica" to ask the Chief's permission. The Chief, seated on a low chair on the rear platform of the car, with a rug over his knees and a magazine in his hand, looked very comfortable and content. Hearing my request, after a moment's thought, he pronounced the idea "rather ridiculous," then remembered it was dangerous as well, and finally asked if I was sure I could hold on. Before the words were well out of his lips, and taking permission for granted by the question, I was again standing by the cow-catcher, admiring the position of the candle-

A CPR pamphlet promoting tours to the Rockies.
Glenbow Archives NA4851-1

Lake Louise

The town of Lake Louise was originally called Laggan, after the Scottish village in Inverness-shire. The name was changed to Lake Louise in 1884, after Queen Victoria's daughter, Princess Louise Caroline Alberta, wife of the man who was then Governor General of Canada.

Previous pages:
KAMLOOPS TO JASPER
Pyramid Lake near Jasper.
Tim Thompson

box, and anxiously asking to be helped on.

Before I take my seat, let me try, briefly, to describe the "Cowcatcher." . . . To begin with, it is misnamed, for it catches no cows at all. Sometimes, I understand, it throws up on the buffer-beam whatever maimed or mangled animal it has struck, but in most cases it clears the line by shoving forward, or tossing aside, any removable obstruction . . .

Behold me now, enthroned on the candle-box, with a soft felt hat well over my eyes, and a linen carriage-cover tucked round me from waist to foot. Mr. E_____ had seated himself on the other side of the headlight. He had succumbed to the inevitable, ceased further expostulation, disclaimed all responsibility, and, like the jewel of a Superintendent he was, had decided on sharing my peril! I turn to him, peeping round the headlight, with my best smile. "This is *lovely*," I triumphantly announce, seeing that a word of comfort is necessary, "quite *lovely*; I shall travel on this cowcatcher from summit to sea!"

Early tourists in the Rockies posing on the cowcatcher of a CPR engine, looking much the same as Agnes Macdonald on her exciting cowcatcher ride.
B.C. Archives and Records Service 43089 B8414

Mr. Superintendent, in his turn, peeps round the headlight and surveys me with solemn and resigned surprise. "I—suppose—you—will," he says slowly, and I see that he is hoping, at any rate, that I shall live to do it!

With a mighty snort, a terribly big throb, and a shrieking whistle, No. 374 moves slowly forward. The very small population of Laggan have all come out to see. They stand in the hot sunshine, and shade their eyes as the stately engine moves on. "It is an awful thing to do!" I hear a voice say, as the little group lean forward; and for a moment I feel a thrill that is very like fear; but it is gone at once, and I can think of nothing but the novelty, the excitement, and fun of this mad ride in glorious sunshine and intoxicating air, with magnificent mountains before and around me, their lofty peaks smiling down on us, and never a frown on their grand faces!

The pace quickens gradually, surely, swiftly, and then we are rushing up to the summit. We soon stand on the "Great Divide"—5300 feet above sea-level—between the two great oceans. As we pass, Mr. E_____ by a

Following pages:
KAMLOOPS TO JASPER
Peyto Lake near Jasper.
Tim Thompson

gesture, points out a small river (called Bath Creek, I think) which, issuing from a lake on the narrow summit-level, winds near the track. I look, and lo! the water, flowing *eastward* towards the Atlantic side, turns in a moment as the Divide is passed, and pours *westward* down the Pacific slope!

Another moment and a strange silence has fallen round us. With steam shut off and brakes down, the 60-ton engine, by its own weight and impetus alone, glides into the pass of the Kicking Horse River, and begins a descent of 2800 feet in twelve miles. We rush onward through the vast valley stretching before us, bristling with lofty forests, dark and deep, that, clinging to the mountain side, are reared up into the sky. The river, widening, grows white with dashing foam, and rushes downwards with tremendous force. Sunlight flashes on glaciers, into gorges, and athwart huge, towering masses of rock crowned with magnificent tree crests that rise all round us of every size and shape. Breathless—almost awe-stricken—but with a wild triumph in my heart, I look from farthest mountain peak, lifted high before me, to the shining pebbles at my feet! Warm wind rushes past; a thousand sunshine colours dance in the air. With a firm right hand grasping the iron stanchion, and my feet planted on the buffer beam, there was not a yard of that descent in which I faltered for a moment. If I had, then assuredly in the wild valley of the Kicking Horse River, on the western slope of the Rocky Mountains, a life had gone out that day! I did not think of danger, or remember what a giddy post I had. I could only gaze at the glaciers that the mountains held so closely, 5000 feet above us, at the trace of snow avalanches which had left a space a hundred feet wide massed with torn and prostrate trees; on the shadows that played over the distant peaks; and on a hundred rainbows made by the foaming, dashing river, which swirls with tremendous rapidity down the gorge on its way to the Columbia in the valley below.

There is glory of brightness and beauty everywhere, and I laugh aloud on the cowcatcher, just because it is all so delightful!

The Glacier Slide

The winter of 1910 saw a series of very heavy snowfalls, resulting in massive avalanches in the Rogers Pass. In spite of the large snowsheds that had been built to protect the CPR main line, snowslides were an unpredictable and extremely frightening hazard. On March 4, as work crews and trains with special rotary

Workers digging out an engine derailed by a snowslide at Rogers Pass, 1897.
Glenbow Archives NA4928-25

plows were clearing a snowslide, a second larger avalanche came down the mountain, instantly killing sixty-two men. It was the worst railway accident in the history of the mountains. The only survivor on that terrible night was Bill LaChance; he later recalled the incredible, nightmarish experience.

I was firing up there then. I was on the helper engine, we lived at Rogers Pass and worked up and down the hill to help trains up . . . My engine was ready to go out and assist a train up the hill, and when we went down to the roundhouse to book out they told us: "That is changed. There's slides down and the trains that are up there are tied up and this engine has got to take the snow plow and go up and clear out them snowslides.

So we hitched onto this rotary plow, and away we went up the hill . . . We had picked up all the crews that were along the road, wintering in outfit cars. We took their sleeping cars and their cooking cars and we took the whole lot up. There was oh, 55 men or so. We bucked right into the snowslides. It had run down and filled the cut, oh, I'd say, maybe 14 feet high. That had just smoothed right over, but it was a messy place because it was full of timber. It had cleaned the hill right off, and it must have run for over a mile down the hill. The rotary would clean it out but then they'd come to logs. So then we'd back up and all these men there with shovels, they'd jump down in that hole that we made—that tunnel in there—and pull out this timber. The timber would break the blades off of the rotary, you see.

So this time we'd backed up and they were all down in there working. Apparently every-

A Canadian Pacific Railway rotary snow plough at Rogers Pass, late 1880s.
Glenbow Archives NA22165-5

123

body was down in that hole. We just backed far enough for them to go down and work. It was along about 11 o'clock at night on March 4, 1910.

The rotary had a big boiler and she had two fire-doors on her, but you always fired through one. But then, as we were just standing there, I opened the two doors and was throwing in coal. The engineer, was standing there with his back to the wind and his window was opened. I leaned over and got a shovelful of coal and just as I brought my eyes back, the flame just come out of that fire from those two doors, just a regular big flame. My goodness! I couldn't think why it had . . .

Of course it was only a fraction of a second until the snow came in across the gangway, and I was right there. Well, it hit me—and how! It took me right out of the gangway and up through the top of that tunnel we had made. I knew it was a snowslide: right then I knew what it was, so I just grabbed my face with my hands.

Well, then the snow got a hold of me and what it didn't do to me. Why, it done everything. It pulled me out twice my length the way it felt, and then it just doubled me all up and rolled me. I was trying to keep rolling up, in a ball to go with the snow. It caught this leg and just turned it around and it would roll me up and stretch me out and double me up. Then the pressure come on, oh, just like as if there were tons on top of me.

Now all the time I am in that I don't get one breath, because the snow was just packed right tight to my face. Then this pressure come on, and things kind of stopped. It just started and it seemed like as it was boiling, and it brought me up out of that heavy pressure. I had about, I suppose, a foot of snow on top of my face. When I threw my hands out, why I had fresh air up there. I dug myself out, and I thought this leg, my right leg, was broken.

Well, it must have all happened pretty fast for the engine because after I got out I couldn't hear the engine. The engine should have been blowing a lot of steam, but there was no sound there. Everything was just dead.

There I was. I'd lost my hat and my gloves were full of snow—we had just little fine gloves, for shovelling—and I took them off and threw them away. My hair was all wet and my mouth was full of blood, and when I spit on the snow there was a great big dark spot on the snow . . . and I thought I'd been hurt inside and I was afraid to put my hands inside of my overalls for fear I'd find my guts laying there. That's the truth. That's just the way I felt . . .

Well, I thought, "Here it is about 11 o'clock at night and it's cold," and the clothes I had on wouldn't wad a gun; just a pair of pant-overalls . . . I was getting kind of cold and so I thought, "Everybody's gone; everybody's passed out" because anybody [that] was in that slide never got a breath of air after they got in it. That snow was just the same as if you took and put your face down into a bag of flour and tried to breathe. That's what the snow was like . . .

. . . Well, it seemed like it was going to be pretty tough that night, if I pulled through it. However, I had to sit there and say my prayers. That's all there was to do.

By gosh, I see a lantern, you know a brakeman's lantern, coming up along there, right along the edge of the slide. By gosh, as soon as I seen that I hollered, and it stopped and looked. I hollered again, and "Who is that's hollering?" he said. And by gosh, it was Johnny Anderson the road foreman. I said "It's Bill LaChance." Oh, he come up and he says, "Bill, where are they all?"

I said , "They're all gone. A man never got a breath of air after he got in and that snow hit them. There's nobody in sight and I've been here quite a little while."

. . . Johnny was standing there in the slide up to pretty near his waist with the loose snow. "Can I carry you off?"

"Why," I said, "you'd do well to walk off. You can't carry me with this snow, and I'm no help."

Well, he said, "I'll give you my mackinaw coat," and he took his mackinaw coat off and give it to me to keep me warm, and away he went . . . he got the cook out of one of the outfit cars and this watchman from the shack down there a mile, and he sent them up to take some blankets and put them on me in the snow so I wouldn't freeze to death. Well, they came up with the blanket—a Chinaman, the cook, and this watchman— and they wanted to cover me up. Well, I said: "There's two slides come down now and I've been in one of them. If another slide comes down I don't want to be rolled up in a blanket. Now," I said, "you get me on that blanket and pull me out of here."

So I hooked that arm over the blanket and there was one on each corner of it and they were doing very good. My jaws were working good; I could hang onto the blanket too with that so they pulled me off and they got me down to where the outfit cars were, off of the slide . . .

A railway snowshed at Rogers Pass in midwinter, with Mount Avalanche in the background, c. 1888.
Glenbow Archives NA4428-22

But anyway the cook had gone and got a cup of tea and brought it to me. And I said to the watchman, "Look at my leg and see if it's hurt." He pulled up my overalls and he got sick.

I said, "Is it bleeding?"

He said, "Something awful."

I said, "Is the blood flowing out or is it shooting out like that?" I wondered if an artery was cut, you see.

"Oh," he says, "it's awful."

I thought, "I don't know. I think time's up pretty good there." The bone was cut right in there, in the shin.

Anyway, he went away and left me there and nobody turned up till daylight. Then they all crowded back up around there and they got me out of this sleeping car, and they took me down and put me in an express car to Glacier. They had a doctor there, Dr. Hamilton. He come in and he took my shoulder and set it back in. They couldn't do very much for that leg because they didn't have any bandages. Somebody said: "What will you have? Would you have a drink of brandy," he said, "or would you have a cup of tea?"

Well, I said, "I'll have a drink of brandy," so they brought me in a cup of tea.

Now I'm all ready to go to town, so they take a rotary and the superintendent's car, and they put the rotary out ahead so if any slides come down, why they'd clean them out as they went down to Revelstoke. But they also sent a message down over the wire that Bill LaChance was the only man that was alive and they didn't expect him to live till he got to Revelstoke . . .

This is what they told me: that the men down in that cut, that whatever they were doing, that's the way they found them. One fellow was standing there holding a torch; another fellow rolling a cigarette. They didn't last long. They never got a breath, and that I know.

The Three Bears

Passengers on board the trains through the mountains are always thrilled at the sight of mountain wildlife. However, train crews in the days of steam often experienced direct encounters with wild animals. Nick Morant, the famous CPR photographer, compiled this story of the hazards of railroading in the national parks of the Rockies, when assistant superintendent George Davis and his co-

worker inadvertently found out what Goldilocks did not know about the three bears.

A 40-car freight, drawn by a 5900 locomotive, eastbound at Lake Louise, was handed orders for a "meet" with three other trains at Castle Mountain siding. The side-tracking, George thought, would give him and his brakeman a wonderful opportunity to make themselves a hot breakfast.

As soon as they were in the siding and the switch safely locked, out came the bacon, the eggs and all the accompanying goodies that were such a feature of caboose life. Soon the surrounding atmosphere was filled with inviting aromas.

Seated at the table, and just about to dig into the fry-pan, the two men felt a movement of the caboose—an effect which always heralds the arrival of a visitor as he swings onto the step. George and his companion expected to see the section foreman or another "brakie," Fred Ramsey, dropping in for coffee. Instead, there loomed in the doorway a large black bear accompanied by two cubs. Hoping to get them off the van, George tried to toss a piece of bread out the doorway but, unfortunately, it struck the wall and bounced back inside. In no time at all that caboose became overcrowded.

The boys took to a built-in escape route—up the ladder into the cupola and out the window onto the roof. From down below, sounds of animal confusion arose—glass being shattered to the accompaniment of growling noises. A glance through the window showed the bears eating the prepared breakfast, one actually sitting in George's chair.

The "meet" completed, the engineer on George's train whistled off and moved onto the mainline with the three bears still holding their ground in the caboose. Brakeman Pawluk, wielding a bamboo rod, was finally able to dislodge the unwelcome guests at a siding at Massive, Alberta.

Van 436432 was a wreck: lamps torn from their wall moorings; broken crockery everywhere; mattresses ripped open, and there remained a pungent reminder that the three bears had passed that way.

An osprey (*Pandion haliaëtus*) above its huge nest.
Chris Steegeri

Opposite page:
A female black bear (*Euarctos americanus*).
Scott Rowed

High Wire Artists

Railway linemen serviced both the trains and the wires that ran along the tracks, carrying the nation's business and gossip. These wires were connected by thousands of poles, which were also used by some birds, like the large osprey, for nesting. Some of these osprey nests can still be seen along the rail line through the mountains. Ken Liddell tells the story of one lineman's battle of wits with these determined birds near Banff.

A lineman's life is not without its humor, however forced his own laughter may be over an incident.

Like all the problems George Scott has had with the osprey. Mr. Scott is a Canadian Pacific lineman at Banff. Two osprey (fish eagles) had him up a pole, literally, for five years.

The persistent birds never heard of the word futility. They would no sooner get to feeling at home in a nest and thinking of drapes and things, than it would become Mr. Scott's duty to tear down the nest which for some reason the osprey took to building on the top crossarm of a pole east of Banff station.

Scott had nothing against the birds, actually he is a lover of birds, but for the life of him he could not see why the osprey would not take the hint and set up housekeeping somewhere else, rather than on a telegraph pole on which they had taken a lease, which Scott, as a servant of some of Canada's biggest companies, was trying to break.

The osprey did not know it, and could have cared less if they had, but what they were doing with their penthouse on a pole was to jeopardize operations of the Calgary-Banff telegraph and teletype circuits, the Trans-Canada network of the Canadian Broadcasting Corporation and facilities of The Canadian Press.

Scott had the strangest of predicaments. The nest kept getting bigger and bigger and when it rained the twigs and things dangled on the wires causing a leak. This was most annoying to the CP Telegraphs, the CBC, and the CP, not to mention Mr. Scott.

When messages and voices became garbled, the wire chief would want to know what the trouble was and Scott had to find it, knowing pretty well it was those osprey again.

The osprey seemed aware of the fact they were protected by National Parks regulations which prevent annoying any of our wild friends. When Scott once asked a warden what he could do about the birds, he may as

White Tail Deer

White tail deer are a reddish chestnut colour and are easily recognized by their foot-long tail, which is white on the underside (hence the name white tail). When running from danger, these deer flick up their tails so the white shows as a signal to other deer and to help fawns follow their mothers in flight. The males weigh up to 275 pounds and their antlers can span up to three feet.

well have asked the osprey.

Scott thought he had the problem licked at one time by rigging wires on the pole in such a way the osprey got a slight shock when they landed. The osprey had an answer for Mr. Scott. Tiring of the daily jerks, the birds simply moved to an adjacent pole.

"If they were owls," Scott remarked at the time, "I'd say they just don't give a hoot."

An osprey is a big bird and it builds a big nest. Some nests Scott knocked down—and he had to do it twice each summer—measured three feet across. These were small nests, too, for osprey. Bird books report the osprey add to a nest from year to year until it can be the size of a small haycock. That, if anything, would be quite a sight to see atop a telegraph pole.

Scott saw the osprey going home with two-foot-long sticks in their beaks. They always hunted up new lumber, never used what he had knocked down. On a crossarm that measures seven inches, they would fashion this stuff into their home with the added ingredients of boughs, moss, dirt and even fair-sized stones. Whether these were to anchor the nest or to throw at Scott, only the osprey knew.

This battle began in 1950 and went on for five years before some ingenious soul came up with the suggestion that a fake crossarm be erected on top of the crossarms that carry the wires.

It worked like a charm and the osprey were welcomed to the site as something of a tourist attraction. But wherever they go in winter, they spread the word about such splendid mountain hospitality.

In 1966 the osprey (nobody knows whether it would be the same pair that had Scott up a pole for so long) returned from their winter quarters with a couple of friends.

Their friends took up an abode on a pole, too, but this one some distance to the west of Banff station, far removed from the original tenants who settled to the east of Banff.

But Scott knew what to do with the newcomers. He simply put a fake crossarm on their pole, too. And everybody was happy, although Scott hoped the osprey weren't going to make a habit of entertaining.

The Most Spectacular
Train Trip in the World

A *century and a half ago, British railway pioneers unleashed a new technology that promised to change the world. As webs of railroads were spun around the globe, the promise was met. Nineteenth-century steam locomotives carried people, freight and dreams—and Canada was one of the dreams delivered by the railway age. Perhaps that fact alone helps to explain the country's continuing love affair with trains.*

In Canada, as elsewhere, the twentieth century's ongoing revolution in transportation posed a persistent threat to the old-fashioned pleasures of train travel. As part of the ambitious modernization programs of the 1950s, both of Canada's major railways converted from steam to diesel-powered engines. The passing of the steam era also marked the dawn of convenient and affordable air transportation;

Opposite page:
Athabasca Falls, a few miles south of Jasper.
Tim Thompson

A Canadian Pacific Railway steam engine with a snow plough, emerging from a snowshed, c. 1910.
Whyte Museum of the Canadian Rockies
V263 NA71-1489

lengthy trips by rail required either the luxury of time or the desire for relaxation and reflection. This was demonstrated by subsequent changes to Canada's passenger rail service.

In an attempt to win back passengers in the age of the plane and automobile, Canadian railways introduced new, streamlined, faster trains with excellent facilities. In 1955 the CPR launched "The Canadian," with its scenic dome cars and faster transcontinental running time. Travellers could now speed across the landscape at 75 miles per hour, sipping a favourite beverage or dining elegantly in air-conditioned comfort, all the while enjoying the captivating scenery which enveloped them. At the same time, the CNR inaugurated "The Super Transcontinental," travelling the northern route through the west via Edmonton and the splendid tourist resort of Jasper.

By 1960 the CPR and CNR shared an almost equal division of the country's total passenger traffic. However, corporate decisions soon dramatically altered this balance. The CPR was convinced that passenger service was hopelessly uneconomic. It reduced "The Canadian" schedule from daily to tri-weekly service and, as traffic decreased, fares were increased. The government-owned CNR, on the other hand, was determined to encourage passenger traffic. Indeed, during the 1960s it emerged at the forefront of passenger rail transportation in North America. By the end of the decade, the CNR was dominant in Canadian passenger traffic, maintaining excellent service and introducing innovative scheduling for "The Super Transcontinental." Nevertheless, passenger services were becoming increasingly unprofitable, and

The two bridges, one belonging to Canadian Pacific and the other to Canadian National, at Cisco Crossings over the Fraser River near Lytton, B.C.
Whyte Museum of the Canadian Rockies
V263 NA71-1574

soon it became clear that Canada's railways would survive only by concentrating on their freight operations. This was confirmed by a 1976 federal government report on the state of railways in Canada.

At this time a vigorous debate took place over whether or not the government was responsible for maintaining passenger rail service. It was agreed that necessary services should continue but that nonessential passenger rail lines would be discontinued. The surviving rail services would then be subsidized by the government. Plans were drawn up for merging the transcontinental services of both the CPR and the CNR into a new government-owned entity: Via Rail Canada, which commenced operations in 1978.

Via Rail introduced a new fare structure and signed operating agree-

Following pages:
Spirit Island in Maligne Lake, the jewel of the Rockies, in Jasper National Park.
Tim Thompson

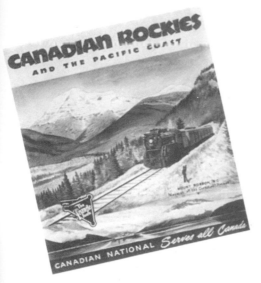

Jasper National Park

*J*asper National Park, established in 1907, is the largest of Canada's mountain parks at 4,200 square miles. The other parks are Banff, Yoho, Glacier and Mount Revelstoke. Significant populations of elk, moose, bighorn sheep and other large animals make Jasper one of the last great wildlife ecosystems remaining in the Rockies.

ments with both railways, allowing passenger trains to use their tracks and maintenance services. "The Canadian" supplanted "The Super Transcontinental" as the single cross-country train. Running on both CPR and CNR tracks, "The Canadian" now followed the rival railways' southern and northern routes through the Rockies. Unfortunately, Via's scheduling had the train running through some of the country's most breathtaking scenery at nighttime. Furthermore, a tightening economy, combined with the constant pressure to cut costs, forced what seemed like continuous cutbacks in service.

In the late 1980s Via Rail undertook a large-scale renovation program and also attempted an experiment in running a daylight-only train through the western mountains—"The Rocky Mountaineer." The strong western Canadian tourist economy consistently generated higher than average passenger traffic, particularly in the summer months. However, after two operating seasons running the "Canadian Rockies by Daylight Service," Via was unable to turn a profit with "The Rocky Mountaineer." In 1989, as part of a larger effort to reduce Via Rail's subsidy, the government decided to privatize this route. The successful bidder was the Great Canadian Railtour Company Ltd., which began operating the train in 1990.

Through a committed management effort and an aggressive international marketing campaign, "The Rocky Mountaineer" has emerged as a successful privately operated train tour, showcasing Canada's Rocky Mountains in all their splendour. Over two days, passengers travel 600 miles in either direction between Vancouver and Jasper, or the Banff/Calgary route. The train ride is solid and smooth: this is the result of welded track that minimizes the clackety-clack sound familiar in movies about railways of the past. In order to ensure that the dramatic mountain vistas are fully enjoyed, the train operates only in daylight, with an overnight stay in historic Kamloops in British Columbia's southern interior.

Through the Fraser Canyon, "The Rocky Mountaineer" follows either CPR or CNR tracks. At Kamloops, the train divides. Part of the train traces the original CPR transcontinental rail line along the route where surveyors and construction crews once struggled against nature and the elements to make such an amazing trip a possibility. This route winds its way through the Rogers Pass to the picturesque resort community of Banff and then on to Calgary. The other option is to travel northward along the North

Thompson River, following the CNR's tracks alongside majestic snow-capped peaks, including Mount Robson, the tallest mountain in the Canadian Rockies, and on to scenic Jasper. Either route constitutes a wonderful journey, which rolls along at an enjoyable pace with plenty of time to marvel at the scenery, wildlife and the outstanding accomplishments of previous generations of pioneering railroaders.

"The Rocky Mountaineer" has justifiably been referred to as "the most spectacular train trip in the world." It has helped to spark a rekindled interest in train travel and an optimism about its prospects in the Canadian west.

More than a century after railways were first built through the Canadian Rockies, passenger trains continue to roll along the famous rail lines that were carved through awe-inspiring mountains and over raging rivers to bind together a new transcontinental nation. Looking ahead into the next century, no one can predict what modes of transportation will carry us to our various destinations. Neither can anyone safely predict how far into the future travel by steel wheels on steel rails will survive. However, in an age of information, where time seems to move at ever-increasing tempos and lives are impossibly hurried, train travel can provide a unique, restful antidote. The rhythm of a journey by train relieves the pressures of our modern age and also provides an opportunity to contemplate our roots, our heritage and the beauty of our land. The dream-inducing spell cast by such a trip has a magnetic quality that draws you in and will not let you go   even after you reach your destination.

It is no wonder that Canadians continue to enjoy travelling by train. Likewise, there is little mystery in why visitors, with the luxury of time, are increasingly attracted to this romantic form of transport. Led by "The Rocky Mountaineer," western Canadians in particular are riding a railway renaissance. Those who do not understand this phenomenon need only go down to the station on the morning of the train's departure to take in the eager anticipation of the milling crowds of passengers and to witness the surge of excitement when the booming voice of the conductor shouts: "All aboard!"

Mount Robson

The highest peak in the Canadian Rockies is Mount Robson, at 12,972 feet. The heavily glaciated north slope drops into Berg Lake and the south side drops into Kinney Lake. The Stoney Indians' name for it is Yuh-hai-has-kun, meaning "the mountain of the spiral road."

The name Robson is actually a shortened form of Robertson. Colin Robertson was an officer of the Hudson's Bay Company in the area, and it is thought that native trappers named the mountain after him. Over the course of time, Robertson was shortened to Robson.

Legend

— *Rocky Mountaineer train routes*
● *Towns and cities*
▲ *Mountains*

1 **2** **3** **4** **5** **6** **7**

Railways break their routes into operating regions called subdivisions. The Rocky Mountaineer route covers four subdivisions on Canadian National Railways tracks (1 to 4) and three on Canadian Pacific Railway tracks (5 to 7). Each subdivision is about 125 miles long and is marked with mileposts, which are white rectangular posts attached to posts and telephone poles. In each sub-division, miles are counted from east to west, and from south to north. Mile 0 is always at the east or south end of the subdivision.

....

Rail distance between

Vancouver and Kamloops	276 miles/ 460 km
Kamloops and Jasper	274 miles/ 457 km
Kamloops and Banff	309 miles/ 515 km
Banff and Calgary	82 miles/ 137 km

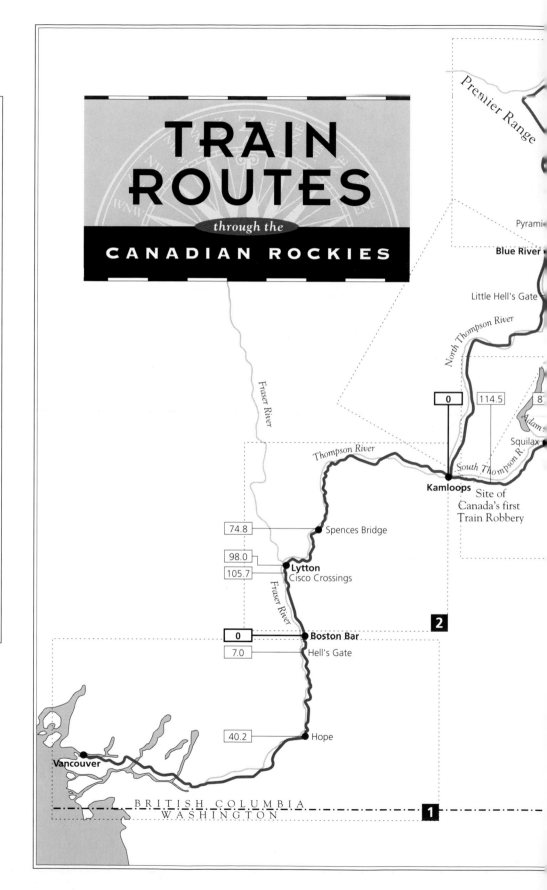

TRAIN ROUTES

through the

CANADIAN ROCKIES

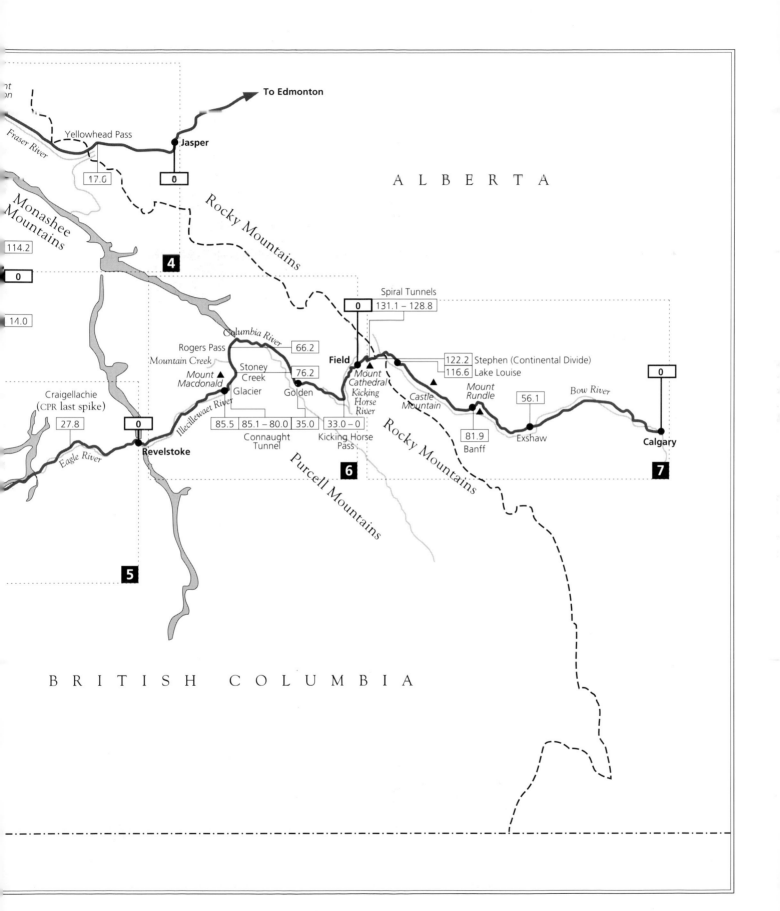

To Edmonton

ALBERTA

Yellowhead Pass

Jasper

17.6

0

Fraser River

Rocky Mountains

Monashee Mountains

114.2

0

14.0

4

Columbia River

Spiral Tunnels

0   131.1 – 128.8

66.2

Rogers Pass

Mountain Creek

Stoney Creek

Mount Macdonald ▲

76.2

Field

Mount Cathedral ▲

122.2   Stephen (Continental Divide)

116.6   Lake Louise

Castle Mountain ▲

Mount Rundle ▲

Bow River

0

Glacier

Golden

Kicking Horse River

56.1

Craigellachie (CPR last spike)

Illecillewaet River

85.5   85.1 – 80.0   35.0   33.0 – 0

Connaught Tunnel

Kicking Horse Pass

81.9

Exshaw

Calgary

27.8

0

Revelstoke

Banff

7

Eagle River

Rocky Mountains

5

Purcell Mountains

6

BRITISH   COLUMBIA

Suggestions for Further Reading

The libraries filled with books on railway heritage are testimony to the enduring popularity of this subject with a wide variety of readers. The following is a select list of available publications that are both useful in providing background or which offer further details of the rich history of western Canada's encounter with railways:

PIERRE BERTON, *The National Dream: The Great Railway, 1871-1881* and *The Last Spike: The Great Railway, 1881-1885* (Toronto: McClelland & Stewart, 1970 and 1971).

BRIAN D. JOHNSON, *Railway Country: Across Canada by Train* (Toronto: Key Porter Books, 1985).

ROBERT F. LEGGETT, *Railways of Canada*, revised edition (Vancouver/Toronto: Douglas & McIntyre, 1987).

DONALD MacKAY, *The Asian Dream: The Pacific Rim and Canada's National Railway* and *The People's Railway: A History of Canadian National* (Vancouver/Toronto: Douglas & McIntyre, 1986 and 1992).

BILL McKEE AND GEORGEEN KLASSEN, *Trail of Iron: The CPR and the Birth of the West, 1880-1930* (Vancouver/Toronto: Douglas & McIntyre in association with Glenbow-Alberta Institute, 1983).

TERRY PINDELL, *Last Train to Toronto: A Canadian Rail Odyssey* (Vancouver/Toronto: Douglas & McIntyre; New York: Henry Holt and Company, Inc., 1992).

R. M. RYLATT, *Surveying the Canadian Pacific: Memoir of a Railroad Pioneer* (Salt Lake City: University of Utah Press, 1991).

BARRIE SANFORD, *The Pictorial History of Railroading in British Columbia* (Vancouver: Whitecap Books, 1981).

SUE SEDDON, *Travel* (Gloucestershire: Alan Sutton Publishing Ltd, 1991).

VIA RAIL CANADA, *Rails Across Canada: 150 Years of Passenger Train History* (Montréal, Via Rail Canada Inc., 1986).

TIMOTHY WHEATON, *The Great Trains: Luxury Rail Journeys of the World* (London: Bison Books, 1990).

Index